MARY ENGELBREIT

WRAP IT UP!
GIFTS TO MAKE
WRAP AND GIVE

Meredith® Press
Des Moines, Iowa

Meredith® Press
An imprint of Meredith® Books

Mary Engelbreit: Wrap It Up! Gifts to Make, Wrap and Give
Editor: Carol Field Dahlstrom
Technical Editor: Susan M. Banker
Graphic Designer: Angie Haupert Hoogensen
Copy Chief: Catherine Hamrick
Copy and Production Editor: Terri Fredrickson
Contributing Proofreaders: Colleen Johnson,
     Margaret Smith, JoEllyn Witke
Technical Illustrator: Chris Neubauer Graphics, Inc.
Electronic Production Coordinator: Paula Forest
Editorial and Design Assistants: Judy Bailey,
     Mary Lee Gavin, Karen Schirm
Production Director: Douglas M. Johnston
Production Manager: Pam Kvitne
Assistant Prepress Manager: Marjorie J. Schenkelberg
Photographers: Peter Krumhardt, Andy Lyons
     Cameraworks, Scott Little
Project Designers: Susan M. Banker, Carol Dahlstrom,
     Phyllis Dunstan, Margaret Sindelar, Alice Wetzel

Meredith® Books
Editor in Chief: James D. Blume
Design Director: Matt Strelecki
Managing Editor: Gregory H. Kayko

Director, Sales & Marketing, Retail:
     Michael A. Peterson
Director, Sales & Marketing, Special Markets:
     Rita McMullen
Director, Sales & Marketing, Home & Garden Center
     Channel: Ray Wolf
Director, Operations: George A. Susral

Vice President, General Manager: Jamie L. Martin

Meredith Publishing Group
President, Publishing Group: Christopher M. Little
Vice President, Consumer Marketing & Development:
     Hal Oringer

Meredith Corporation
Chairman and Chief Executive Officer: William T. Kerr

Chairman of the Executive Committee: E. T. Meredith III

Cover Illustration: Mary Engelbreit Studios

All of us at Meredith® Press are dedicated to providing you with information and ideas to create beautiful and useful projects. We welcome your comments and suggestions. Write to us at: Meredith® Press, Crafts Editorial Department, 1716 Locust St., Des Moines, IA 50309-3023.

If you would like to purchase copies of any of our books, check wherever quality books are sold.

 is a registered trademark of Mary Engelbreit Enterprises, Inc.

LOOK FOR THESE CRAFT TITLES FROM MARY ENGELBREIT:

Put Your Heart in It!

The heart of the giver makes the gift dear and precious. —LUTHER

Giving gifts is such a simple gesture and yet it is so rewarding—more rewarding than receiving gifts. I truly believe this. Oddly enough, we discover that the most rewarding gifts are the ones we spend a little more time seeking out, the ones we wrapped with detail, and gifts that are handmade—these are the special gifts that come from the heart.

This book is a wonderful source of just these types of gifts—with unique gift ideas and creative ways to wrap and present them—for any occasion. Fill a decoupage tin with get-well goodies for a dear friend under the weather. Decorate a straw hat with colorfully painted garden tools as a housewarming gift. Paint and fill a wagon full of toys for a little one. You'll also discover an array of unique holiday gift ideas to make the season of giving even more special.

And for those last-minute events and afterthoughts, you'll be prepared with the quick-to-make gift ideas that we've created—a bon voyage bag filled with travel goodies, or a creative way to present a gift subscription.

Remember, gifts come in a variety of shapes, sizes, and packages, but all gifts come from the heart!

Enjoy!

Mary Engelbreit

contents

CHAPTER 1 It's a Special Occasion

Celebrate the special moments in the lives of the ones you love with memorable gifts you can make with love and give with pride.

CHAPTER 2 For Dear Friends

Show your appreciation for treasured friendships with these sweet tokens of affection.

CHAPTER 3 Last-Minute Gifts

While these meaningful gifts may look like they took a lot of time, you can pull them together quickly with just a few easy-to-find supplies.

CHAPTER 4 Breit Ideas for the Holidays

Giving gifts at Christmastime brings so much joy, and these festive crafts will have you feeling like the jolly ol' elf himself.

CHAPTER 5 Gifts of Goodies

From mugs and boxes to bowls of all shapes and sizes, these clever containers are perfect for sharing gifts from the kitchen.

CHAPTER 6 Presents for the Children

Make a child's day bright with fun-to-make, fun-to-give gifts they'll remember forever.

CHAPTER 7 Fun-to-Make Bows

The perfect finishing touch, these whimsical bows will add sparkle to every gift you give.

it's a special occasion

Extend sincere "congratulations," or a cheerful "good for you," with a meaningful gift you create with artistic flair. Arrive at a birthday party with a money-filled frame the guest of honor will adore. Accompany best wishes for new parents with decorative stacking boxes filled with gifts for baby. Say "Happy Mother's Day," with a toolbox mom will use and treasure always. The inspiration is endless in this oh-so-clever present-filled chapter.

Sweet Sixteen Frame

Whether filled with several bills or a five, ten, or twenty—this vivid frame, with its sure-to-be appreciated stash of cash, will be loved by kids of any age.

WHAT YOU'LL NEED FOR THE TAG

Tracing paper
Pencil
Scissors
Medium-weight papers in red and yellow
Round paper punch
Glue stick
Mary Engelbreit® sticker of choice
Black fine-line marker
Black cord

HERE'S HOW

1. Trace the heart patterns, *page 110*, onto tracing paper and cut out. Trace around the small heart on red paper and the large heart on yellow. Cut out.
2. Punch a hole in the top of the yellow heart, about ⅛ inch from the edge. Glue the red heart atop the yellow heart. Affix the sticker at the top of the red heart.
3. Use the marker to add dots around the yellow border. Write desired message in tag center.
4. Insert the cord through the hole.

WHAT YOU'LL NEED FOR THE FRAME

White spray primer
Wooden frame
Acrylic paints in medium blue, light green, yellow, red, coral, black, and white
Paintbrushes
Four 1-inch-wide wooden hearts
Four ½-inch wide wooden hearts
Clear water-based varnish
Wood glue
Black fine-line marker
Picture mat
Bills to denote the age of the person
Clear tape
1½-inch wide wooden heart
2½-inch-wide pin back
Ribbon

HERE'S HOW

1. Prime the surface of the frame with a light coat of white spray primer.
2. Paint the frame various colors, using the grooves in the frame as a guide. Paint stripes, checks, or flowers. To paint flowers, dip the handle end of a paintbrush in paint and dot on petals. Paint the eight small wooden hearts, including edges, in a contrasting color. Use a fine-pointed brush to make lines as shown. Let the paint dry.
3. Varnish all pieces and let them dry. Layer the small hearts on top of the larger ones, using a small amount of wood glue to hold them together. Glue the pieces onto the frame and let dry.
4. Use the marking pen to write "Happy Birthday Sweet 16!" and small hearts on the picture mat.
5. Arrange 16 one-dollar bills (or the desired configuration of bills) to fit within the picture mat. Gently tape the bills on the very edges (so that the tape will not be seen). Place the glass, mat, and mounted bills into frame. Replace the back of the frame.
6. To make the Sweet 16 pin, paint the large wooden heart red. Let it dry. Write the words "Sweet 16" or whatever you wish. Let it dry. Apply a coat of varnish and let dry. Apply a second coat of varnish. Let it dry. Attach a pin back with glue. Let it dry.
7. Tie ribbon around the frame as if wrapping a gift. Affix the pin to the ribbon.

9

Have-a-Heart Valentine Tin

Tell someone how sweet you think they are by sending a hidden trove of candy conversation hearts in a clever keepsake tin.

Both sides of this tin have been decoupaged using a variety of cutout motifs.

WHAT YOU'LL NEED

Small metal lunch box or metal tin
Masking tape
White flat spray paint
Acrylic paints in red, yellow, and black
Paintbrush
Scissors
Greeting cards and decorative envelopes
Mod Podge decoupage medium

HERE'S HOW

1. Wash and dry the lunch box or tin. Wrap the handle with masking tape to protect it from getting paint on it. Spray the outside surfaces with white spray paint. Let the paint dry. If necessary, apply a second coat and let dry.

▶ **2.** Using the photographs, *left* and *opposite*, for inspiration, paint the separated areas in red, yellow, and black as desired. Let the paint dry.

▶ **3.** To decoupage designs onto the box or tin, cut out selected motifs from greeting cards or envelopes. Coat the back side of the paper with a generous coat of decoupage medium. Position the pieces on the tin surface and press out any wrinkles and excess decoupage medium. Let the decoupage medium dry.

4. Coat all of the painted and decoupaged surfaces with a final coat of decoupage medium, covering all surfaces. Remove the tape from the handle.

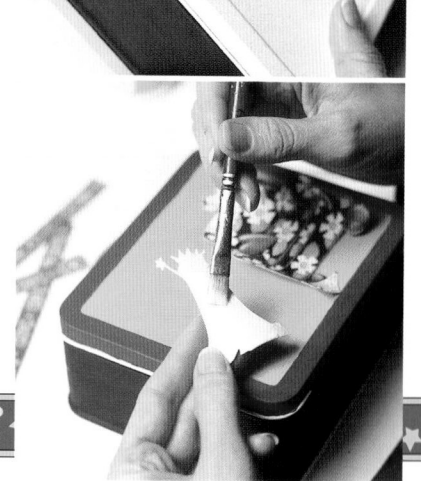

Queen-for-a-Day Crown

Pamper a pal or loved one with favorite bath items and aromatic sprays brimming from a golden crown that's fit for a queen.

WHAT YOU'LL NEED FOR THE TAG

Medium-weight papers in yellow and blue
Two different decorative-edged scissors
Glue stick
Star-shaped paper punch
Mary Engelbreit's® "The Queen Has Spoken" sticker
3/16-inch-wide red velvet ribbon
Red fine-line marker

HERE'S HOW

1. Cut a 3¼x2-inch rectangle from yellow paper using one of the decorative-edged scissors. Using the other scissors, cut a 1x2¼-inch strip from blue. Glue the blue strip atop the yellow rectangle, approximately ¾ inches from the left edge.
2. Use the star-shaped paper punch to create two star shapes in the lower right corner and one in the upper left corner.
3. Affix the sticker over the blue paper strip.
4. Thread the ribbon through the star-shaped hole in the upper left corner. Write desired message in the large yellow area.

WHAT YOU'LL NEED FOR THE CROWN

Tracing paper and pencil
Scissors
5x26-inch piece of gold felt
5x26-inch piece of red felt
3x3-inch piece of red felt
8x8-inch piece of red felt
8-inch round cardboard container
Thick white crafts glue
Metallic gold paint pen
Paintbrush
Foam plate
Six 1-inch-high oval gems, two each of teal, blue, and red
Fourteen ¼-inch round red gems
26-inch-long piece of red braid
Crinkle-cut paper strips
Bath gift items

HERE'S HOW

1. Trace the patterns, *pages 14-15*, onto tracing paper and cut out. (NOTE: The wavy lines do not indicate cut lines. These strips wrap to the back of the crown and should be cut the entire length of the felt strip.) Trace around the patterns on the gold felt and red felt pieces, extending the back joining strips. Cut the "Q" from red felt. Trace around the bottom of the cardboard container on the 8x8-inch piece of red felt. Cut out all felt shapes.
2. Align the bottom of the cardboard container with the bottom of the crown pattern used to cut the gold felt. Trace around the pattern on the container. Cut out the crown shape, approximately ⅛ inch inside of the traced lines.
3. Align and glue the gold felt to the outside of the cardboard container, overlapping the edges. Align and glue the red crown shape to the inside of the cardboard container. Let the glue dry.
4. Put some gold paint on a plate and lightly paint the surface of the gold felt. Let the paint dry.
5. Center the "Q" cut from red felt on the front of the crown.
6. On the back side of the large oval gems, apply a ring of paint pen close to the edge. Carefully press the gems in place.
7. Place seven pea-sized dots of paint pen on each side of the "Q", every ¾ inch. Carefully press a small round gem onto each dot of paint. Let the paint pen dry.
8. Glue braid around the bottom. Fill the crown with crinkle-cut paper and desired bath items.

Center

queen-for-a-day gold
felt crown pattern

queen-for-a-day "Q" pattern

14

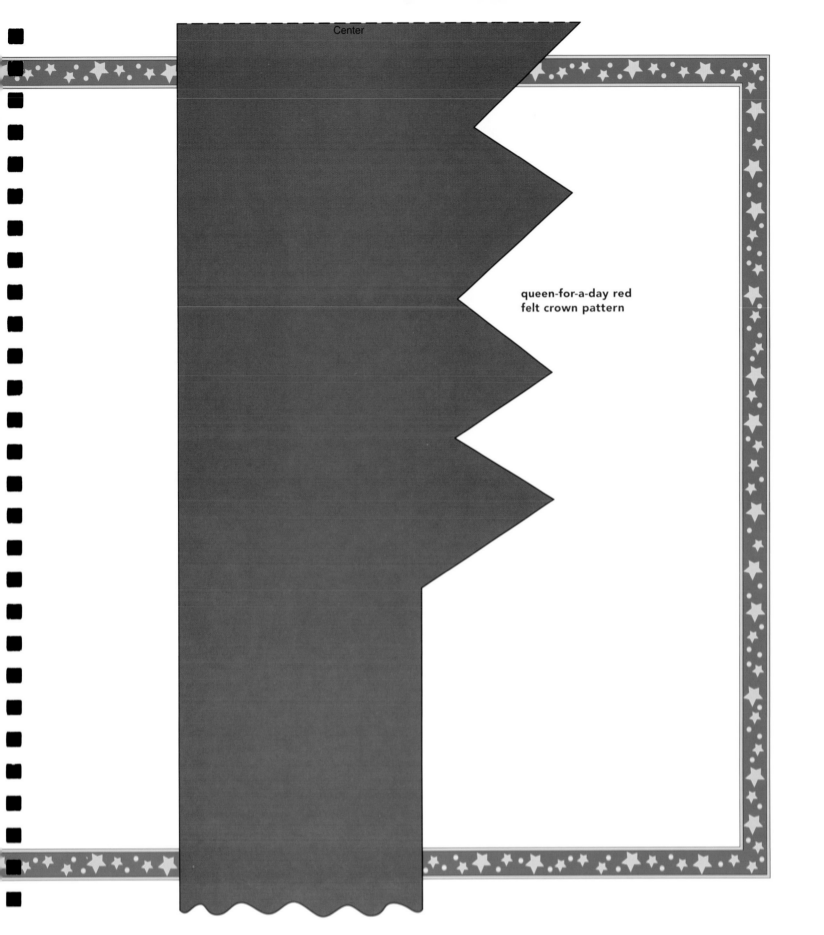

Center

queen-for-a-day red
felt crown pattern

Precious Baby Blocks

Perfect for holding gifts for a sweet newborn, these blocks double as stacking and nesting toys as baby grows.

WHAT YOU'LL NEED FOR THE TAG

Medium-weight papers in pink and white print, mint green, white, lavender, and light yellow
Scissors and pinking shears
Glue stick
Star and round paper punches
Purple fine-line marker
⅛-inch-wide ribbon

HERE'S HOW

1. Cut a 4-inch square from print paper. Cut a 3-inch square from mint green. Cut a 2½-inch square from white using pinking shears. Cut a 2-inch square from lavender. Cut a 1¾-inch square from yellow.
2. Glue the squares atop each other in descending size order.
3. Punch four lavender stars. Glue in corners of yellow square. Punch a hole in one corner. Write a message in center. Push ribbon through the hole.

WHAT YOU'LL NEED FOR THE BLOCKS

3 cardboard boxes in graduated sizes
Acrylic paints in very pale peach, medium soft peach, pale lavender, medium lavender, yellow, very pale yellow, dark pink, medium pink, very pale pink, very pale blue, medium pastel blue, white, grass green, very pale green, and medium pastel green
Paintbrushes
Ruler and pencil
Tracing paper; scissors
One sheet of crafting foam
Thick white crafts glue
Pencil with eraser for painting
Black fine-point permanent marker
3 yards of wide ribbon

HERE'S HOW

1. Paint all the outside surfaces of the boxes and lids with white paint. Allow the paint to dry. Place the lid on the box and draw a light pencil line on the box where it meets lid. (This guide will be the top line of the squares on each side of the box.)
2. Measure the width of the lid edge. Use this measurement to draw a square border on each side of the box and on the top of the lid.
3. Paint in solid areas. Paint the very light pastel colored borders

first. Paint the large box pale blue, the medium box pale green, and the small box pale yellow, as shown at *right*.
4. Paint the square blocks on each panel with desired colors. Paint the lids in the same manner.
5. Create a stamping tool for small, simple shapes. You may use the heart and triangle patterns provided. Trace onto fun foam or draw your own. Cut out the small shape of fun foam and glue it to the unused eraser end of a pencil or end of a dowel. Let it dry firmly. Dip your little stamping tool in paint and dot it onto the surface to be stamped.
6. On the large blue box, add random large and small dots in the pale blue border. Dip the handle end of a brush into paint and dot onto surface. Paint the darker yellow vertical stripes over the pale yellow using a small narrow brush.
7. Trace the heart pattern onto tracing paper, cut it out, and trace onto the box. Paint hearts medium pink. Do the same also with the letter C. Paint opposite sides and lid with a heart. The other two sides should have alphabet letters.

(continued on page 18)

for
Sweet
Baby
Emma

8. Paint soft green stripes in the green box border. Then stamp the small pink hearts onto the pale pink background. Allow them to dry. Next trace the star and letters onto two opposite sides each. Paint these yellow. Make pink dots on the stars.

9. For the smallest box, add the triangular patterns in the lavender border using a triangle stamp. Make the little peach dots in the pale peach background, making tiny dots in groups of three. To make dots, use a small paintbrush and dip the handle end in paint, then dot onto surface. Paint the letters and flowers again, alternating letters opposite sides and flowers on opposite sides and top.

10. When all of the paint is dry, outline the areas as desired with a fine-point black permanent marker.
11. Fill the boxes with baby gifts and stack them large to small. Tie the pyramid with a long piece of wide ribbon, adding a bow on top.

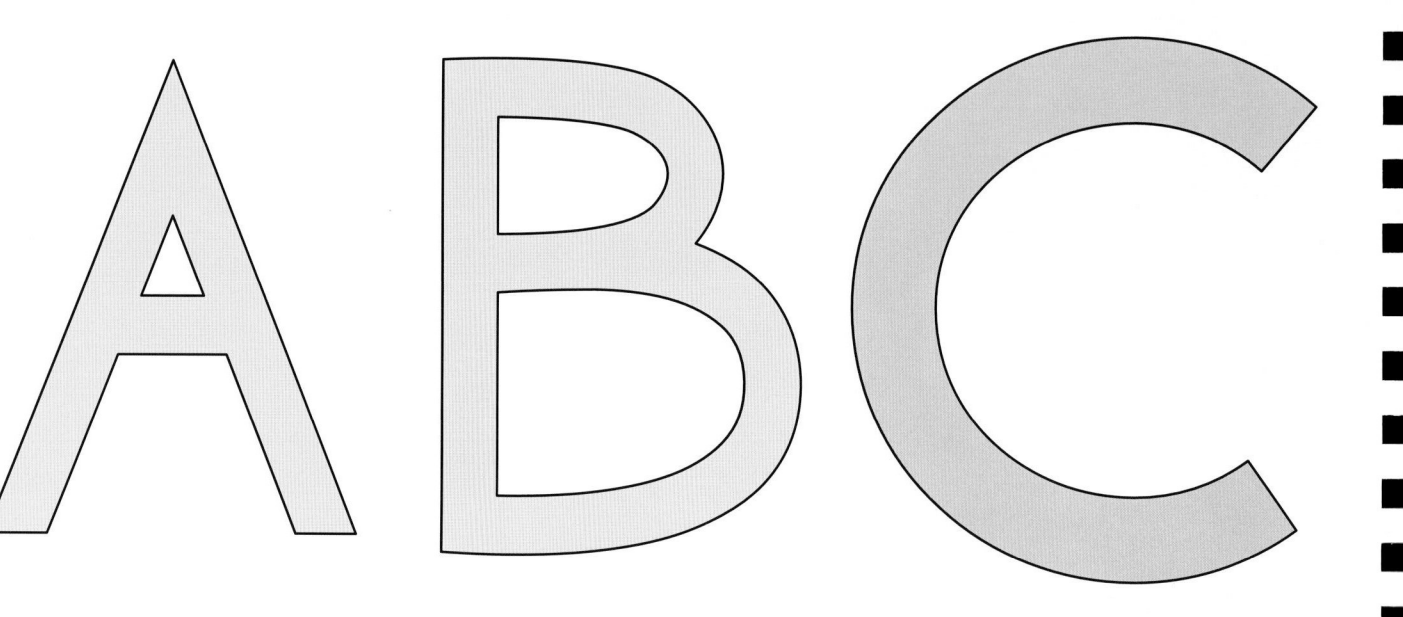

precious baby blocks patterns

Sweetly-Painted Vase

WHAT YOU'LL NEED FOR THE TAG

Medium-weight pink and white papers
White paper doily
Scissors
Thick white crafts glue
Decorative-edged scissors
Paper punch
Small pink satin ribbon rose
⅛-inch gold cording
Metallic gold marker

HERE'S HOW

1. Cut a 3½x2¾-inch piece from pink and white papers and from doily. Using decorative-edged scissors, trim the white paper ¼ inch from all sides.

2. Glue the doily piece atop the pink paper. Center and glue the white paper atop the doily.

3. Use a paper punch to make a hole in the center of one short edge of tag. Glue the rose to the opposite side.

4. Thread the cording through the hole. Write the desired message in the center of the tag.

Filled with dainty pink roses, this lovely vase paints up quickly to hold a bouquet for Grandma or a special Auntie.

WHAT YOU'LL NEED FOR THE VASE

Rosebud vase
Paintbrush
Pink, green, and white glass paints
Gold glitter dimensional paint pen
Assorted pink and green beads
Gold cord

HERE'S HOW

1. Wash and dry the vase. Avoid touching the areas to be painted.

2. To paint flowers around the vase where shown, *opposite*, dip the handle end of a paintbrush into the paint and dot it onto the surface of the vase. When the paint is dry, dot a smaller white dot in the center of each flower. Paint small green leaves at the top and bottom of each flower.

3. Bake the painted vase in the oven if instructed by the paint manufacturer. Let the vase cool.

4. Paint designs on the vase as desired by making dots with the glitter paint pen. Let the paint dry.

5. String beads onto the cord and knot the cord ends. Tie the cord around the neck of the vase.

We love you Auntie Katie

Mom's Toolbox

Help mom be even handier with a bright floral toolbox she can call her own!

WHAT YOU'LL NEED FOR THE TAG

Tracing paper
Pencil
Scissors
Medium-weight papers in black and yellow
Glue stick
Round paper punch
Red fine-line marker
Black cord

HERE'S HOW

1. Trace the hammer pattern, *page 110*, onto tracing paper. Cut out shape. Trace around the hammer on black paper and the handle portion only on yellow paper. Cut out the shapes.
2. Glue the yellow handle atop the black handle. Punch a hole in the end of the handle, about ¼ inch from the edge.
3. Use the marker to add ⅛-inch stripes to each end of the handle as shown. Write desired message between the stripes.
4. Thread the cord through the punched hole.

WHAT YOU'LL NEED FOR THE TOOLBOX

Red metal toolbox
Thick white crafts glue
3 yards each of black and white cord
Scissors
Acrylic enamel paints in black, white, yellow, green, lavender, and red
½-inch flat paintbrush
Pencil and ⅝-inch dowel
Tracing paper
Tools such as a hammer, screwdriver, tape measure, pliers, and jars for tacks, nails, and screws
Sheets of crafting foam in green, yellow, and lavender

HERE'S HOW

1. To cover the handle of the toolbox, coat it with glue. Cut 10-inch lengths of black and white cord. Starting on the underside of the handle, wind one color of cord around the handle several times and trim it so that it ends on the underside of the handle. Continue wrapping the handle with cord, alternating colors.
2. Paint a 2-inch high band of white around the bottom of the toolbox. It may require two or three coats to cover well. Allow the paint to dry.
3. Use a pencil to draw faint lines every inch to make two rows of checks. Paint every other square

black with a flat brush. Alternate the black squares on the second row.
4. To paint the round flowers on the toolbox lid, paint a circle, or make a dot by using a small length of ⅝-inch dowel. Dip it in paint and dot it onto the surface. To make the small center dot, dip the handle end of a paintbrush into paint and dot it on the flower center. Paint on simple round green leaves. To make the other flowers, trace the flower pattern, *below*, onto tracing paper and cut it out. Trace around the pattern where desired on the lid. Paint these flowers lavender and let dry. Paint a yellow center and green leaves.
5. If desired, decorate the tool handles. The handles may be plastic, wood, metal, or rubber-coated. Use an acrylic enamel paint if paint is desired. Paint desired motifs such as dots, stripes, or solid areas.
6. Paint jar lids solid colors. Cut out circles from crafting foam to make flowers, and ovals to make leaves. Glue the shapes onto the lids and a pull-out tape measure.

flower pattern for tool box

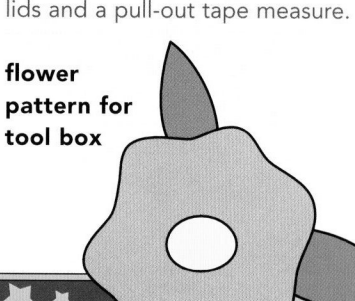

for dear
friends

Friendship—one of life's most cherished rewards—is the focus in this warm-hearted chapter. To celebrate those special people who bring so much joy, we've created projects you can make and give with love. From painted bowls brimming with goodies to a keepsake bag made from woven ribbons, you'll find the perfect gifts to craft for friends dear at heart.

Get-Well Wishes

MORE GIFT-GIVING IDEAS

This fun idea can be used for nearly every occasion. Simply select a suitable greeting card to decoupage on the tin and fill with coordinating items. Here are some ideas:

- Fill a tin with coasters and pretty napkins for a housewarming.
- Tuck baby shampoo, bath wash, and pacifiers in a tin for a newborn.
- Fill a tin with monogrammed toasting glasses to congratulate the newlyweds.

Someone who's under the weather will be feeling better quickly with this fun tin filled with everything from chicken soup to aspirin.

WHAT YOU'LL NEED

Small tin box
Flat white spray paint
Acrylic paints in black, white, and red; paintbrush
Greeting card
Scissors
Mod Podge decoupage medium
Ribbon and bow
Thick white crafts glue
Chicken noodle soup, aspirin, tea, cough drops, bandages, Mary Engelbreit's® *Take Good Care* book, or other "get-well" items

HERE'S HOW

1. Clean and dry the tin box. Spray the tin with two to three light coats of white paint. Allow the paint to dry.
2. Paint the background area on the lid with black. Allow it to dry. Paint the bottom portion of the tin with red.
3. Trim the card to the desired size to fit the top of the tin. Coat the back of the card with a generous amount of decoupage medium. Position the card on the lid and smooth out the wrinkles. Let it dry.
4. Add white dots on the remaining black surface by dipping the handle end of a paintbrush in white paint and dotting it onto the surface. Let the paint dry.
5. Coat the lid with decoupage medium. Glue a ribbon around the middle of the tin bottom. Glue a bow over the ribbon where desired. Fill the tin with "get-well" items.

Colorful Sewing Bird

This bluebird pincushion, complete with a needle sharpener, has embroidered wings made with colorful variegated floss.

MORE GIFT-GIVING IDEAS

To give this colorful sewing accessory to a special seamstress, tuck the bluebird into a basket "nest." To add even more color and texture, fill the nest with any of the following:

- Skeins of embroidery floss
- Spools of thread
- Small cuts of calico
- Rolls of felt squares
- Buttons and beads
- Antique thimble
- Needlepoint yarns

WHAT YOU'LL NEED

Tracing paper and pencil
Scissors
¼ yard of blue coating wool
4x4-inch piece of blue felted imitation suede fabric for wings
Cardboard
Green checked fabric scrap
Green felt scrap
Pinking shears
Variegated embroidery floss
Thread and needle
Polyester fiberfill
Fusible interfacing
Yellow embroidery floss
2 tiny black buttons for eyes
Grit removed from used or purchased needle sharpener

HERE'S HOW

1. Trace the patterns, *pages 30–31*, onto tracing paper and cut out. Transfer the bird pattern to the wool, the wing pattern to the suede twice (reversing one), and the base pattern to the cardboard and to the wool. Cut the needle sharpener from green checked fabric and the topper from green felt.

2. Cut the oval base shape from the cardboard. Cut all other pieces ¼ inch outside the pattern markings for the seam allowance. Use pinking shears to cut the wings.

3. Add decorative chain stitches, *page 31*, to the wings as shown using three plies of floss. Stitch the wings to the bird's sides, leaving the top edge open for a pocket.

4. Stitch the sides together, leaving the bottom open. Trim and clip the seams. Turn and stuff with fiberfill.

5. Fuse the wool to the cardboard. Handstitch the bottom to the bird.

6. Use yellow embroidery floss to add the beak in straight stitches and French knots (see diagrams on *page 31*). Sew on the eyes.

7. Fold the checked fabric for the needle sharpener in half and sew as shown on the pattern. Fill with sharpener grit and sew the felt topper over the open edges.

8. For twisted cord, cut four 4-yard pieces of floss. Knot one end and tape to a suitable surface. Twist the opposite end until the cord kinks back on itself. Fold the twisted cord in half and let it wind around itself. Attach one end to the green checked needle sharpener and the center to the bird's back.

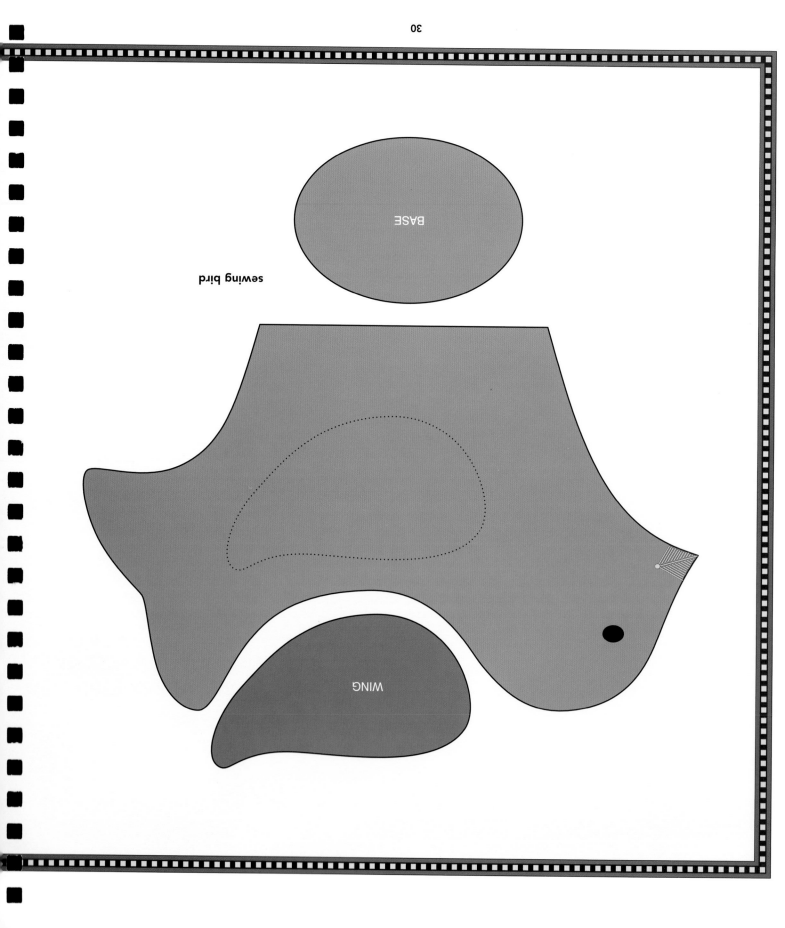

sewing bird

BASE

WING

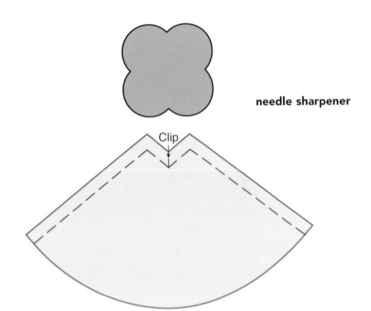

needle sharpener

Clip

chain stitch

french knot

satin stitch

Woven Ribbon Bag

WHAT YOU'LL NEED FOR THE TAG

Medium-weight yellow paper
Pinking shears
Ruler
Pencil
Paper punch
¼-inch-wide polka-dot ribbons
   in black-and-white and
   red-and-white
Black marker

HERE'S HOW

1. Cut a 2x3½-inch rectangle using pinking sheers.
2. Measure and mark every ½ inch along the long edges of paper, approximately ½ inch from paper edge. Measure and mark two holes on each end of tag, centered and ½ inch apart. Use a paper punch to make a hole at each marking.
3. Cut two 4½-inch lengths of red-and-white ribbon. Cut a 3-inch length from black-and-white ribbon. Cut a second length measuring 11 inches.
4. Weave the red-and-white ribbons through the holes in the tag at the top and bottom. Weave the short black-and-white ribbon through the right-hand end. Weave the long black-and-white ribbon through the left-hand end, leaving a loop in the top for a hanger.
5. Write the desired message in the center of the tag.

Pretty enough to hold a gift of jewelry, this bright woven bag could also be used for cosmetics, tissues, or traveling.

WHAT YOU'LL NEED FOR THE WOVEN BAG

Scissors
¼ yard of lightweight fusible
   interfacing
Pins
Corrugated cardboard or
   foam-core board
Approximately 9 yards of desired
   ribbon, ¼- to 1½-inches wide

Fusible hemming tape and iron
7x19-inch piece of lining fabric
Thread to match ribbons
Snap and button
Decorative pin

(continued on pages 34–35)

HERE'S HOW

1. Cut a 6½x18½-inch piece of interfacing. Pin the interfacing, fusible side up, to the cardboard.

▼ **2.** Cut enough 18½-inch-long ribbons to cover the interfacing. Pin the ribbons side by side atop the interfacing as shown.

▼ **3.** Cut several ribbons to a length of 6½ inches. Pin fusible hem tape to the ribbon backs.

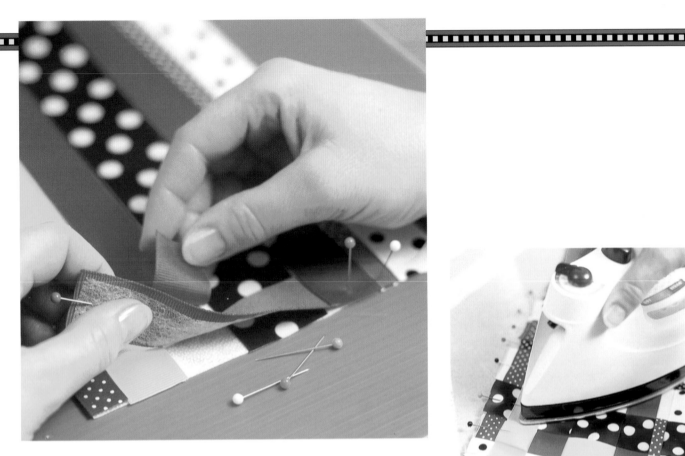

▲ **4.** Begin weaving short ribbons with those pinned to the cardboard.
▼ **5.** Pin the ribbon ends as the weaving is completed.

▶ **6.** Using an iron, fuse the ribbons to the interfacing, removing the pins as you go. Trim the edges even if necessary.

7. Place the lining fabric atop the woven ribbon piece, right sides facing. Stitch together using a ¼-inch seam allowance and leaving one short end open. Trim seams and turn.

8. Measure 4½ inches from stitched short end. Fold the woven piece at this point with right sides facing. Hand-stitch both side seams. Turn right side out.

9. To make the flap point, measure 2½ inches from open end on each side. Fold the corners together and stitch from marked sides to center of flap. Turn right side out.

10. Sew on a snap closure where flap point meets the bag. Sew a button and decorative pin to the point of the flap.

Sentiments in Suede

Give someone special a token of your love by sharing these striking stitched hearts tucked into delicate, button-embellished envelopes.

WHAT YOU'LL NEED FOR THE TAG

Tracing paper and pencil
Crafting foam in red and purple
Scissors and pinking shears
Thick white crafts glue
Green button and embroidery floss
10-inch piece of ¼-inch-wide ribbon
Black fine-line marker

HERE'S HOW

1. Trace the heart patterns, *page 111*, onto tracing paper. Cut out and trace around small heart on red foam and the large heart on purple. Cut out the red heart using scissors, the purple using pinking shears.
2. Glue the small heart atop the large heart.
3. Sew a button to the top of the red heart, catching the center of the ribbon on the backside. Knot the ribbon ends.
4. Write a message in the center of the tag.

WHAT YOU'LL NEED FOR THE SUEDE HEARTS

Tracing paper and pencil
Scissors and pinking shears
7x7-inch piece of felted imitation suede fabric in desired color for backing and a 6x6-inch piece of felted imitation suede fabric in a complementary color
Small pieces of felted imitation suede fabric for flowers and leaves
Fusible interfacing
Variegated embroidery floss in desired colors and tape
Paper punch
Vintage buttons

HERE'S HOW

1. *For the hearts:* Trace patterns, *pages 38–39*, onto tracing paper and cut out. Use the patterns to cut shapes from the desired colors of suede, cutting large heart with pinking shears. Cut additional flower, leaf, and small heart shapes from fusible interfacing. Fuse flower and leaf shapes to the small heart with interfacing between the heart and the flower shapes.
2. Embroider all details using three plies of floss and blanket stitches and backstitches.

3. Fuse the embroidered heart to the backing piece of suede. Use pinking shears to trim backing fabric approximately ⅛ inch from the heart.
4. For 18 inches of twisted cord, cut three 2-yard pieces of floss. Knot one end and tape to a suitable surface. Twist the opposite end until the cord kinks back on itself. Fold the twisted cord in half and let it wind around itself.
5. Use a paper punch to make a hole in the top of heart. Lace cord through the hole and tie a bow.
6. Sew a vintage button to the flower center, if desired.

WHAT YOU'LL NEED FOR THE ENVELOPES

Glassine paper
Pencil
Scissors
Pinking shears
Glue stick
Super Glue gel
Needle
Embroidery floss
Buttons

(continued on page 38)

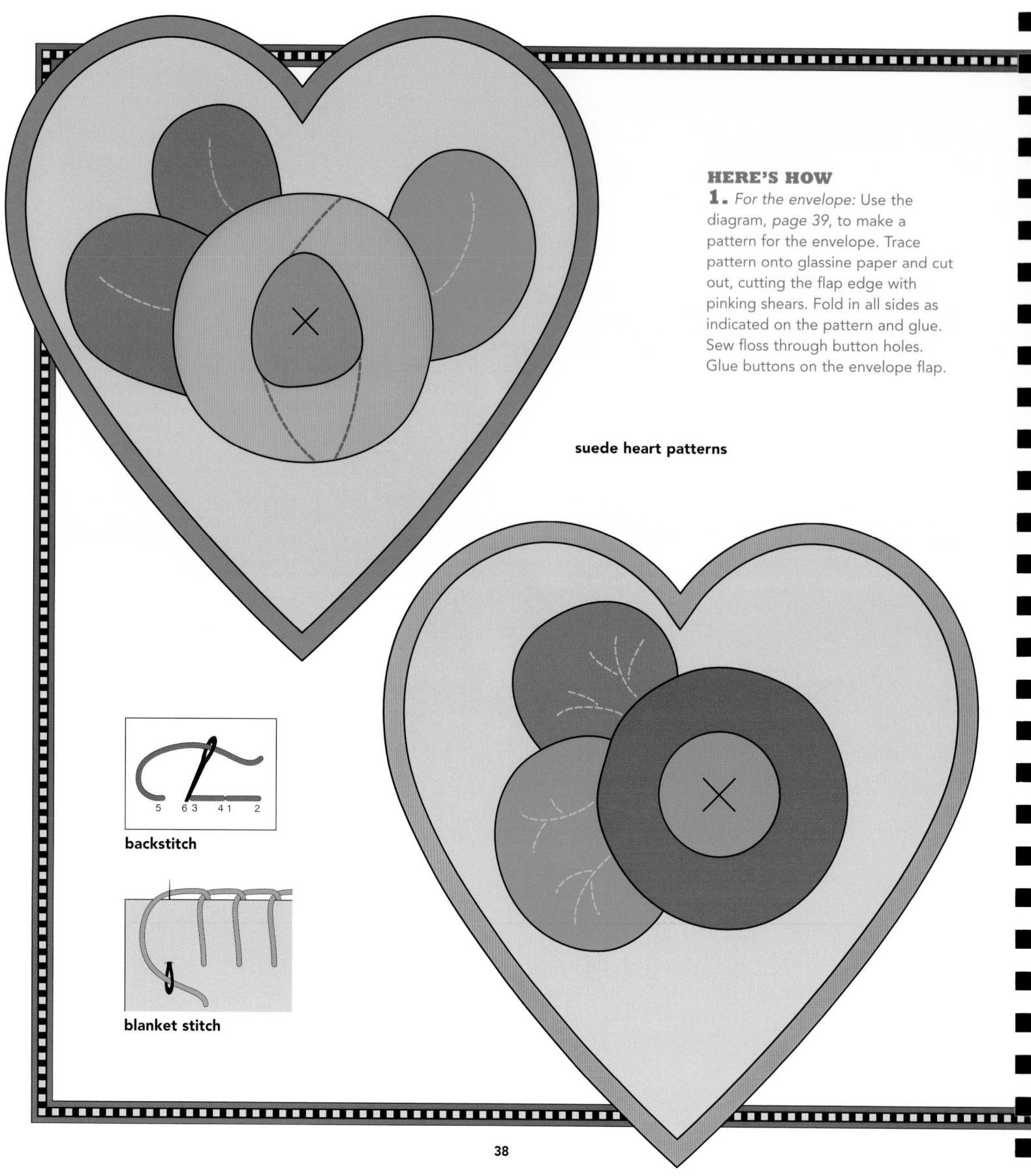

HERE'S HOW

1. *For the envelope:* Use the diagram, *page 39,* to make a pattern for the envelope. Trace pattern onto glassine paper and cut out, cutting the flap edge with pinking shears. Fold in all sides as indicated on the pattern and glue. Sew floss through button holes. Glue buttons on the envelope flap.

suede heart patterns

backstitch

blanket stitch

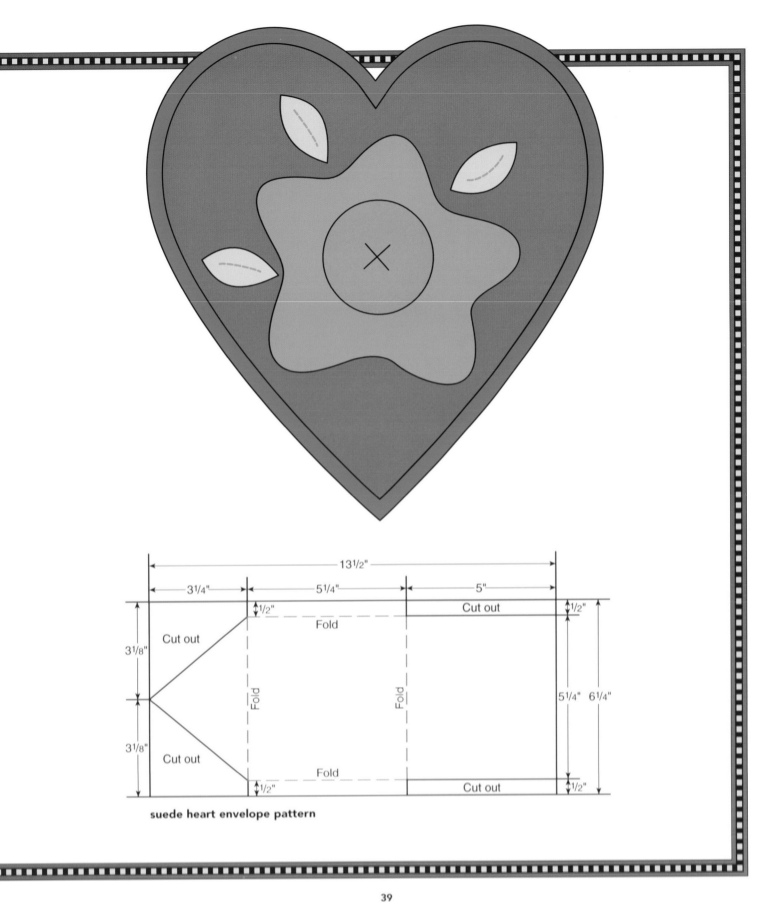

suede heart envelope pattern

Good Cook's Apron

MORE GIFT-GIVING IDEAS

When you purchase an apron for your favorite cook, pick up an extra or two! This easy-appliqué, easy-paint apron has other possibilities as well:

- Appliqué "Artist at Work" along with paintbrushes for an aspiring painter.
- Keep a gardener's clothes free of potting soil with a flower-laden apron.
- Trim an apron with cloth appliqués of tools for a beloved woodworker.

Something great is cooking—this fun-to-make, fun-to-wear apron makes an unexpected "wrap" for a favorite cookbook.

WHAT YOU'LL NEED

Purchased gold apron
Iron
Fusible webbing
Assorted solid and calico cotton scraps
  Pencil; tracing paper
  Scissors
    Acrylic paints in black and white
      Paintbrush

HERE'S HOW

1. Wash, dry, and press a purchased apron.

2. To prepare fabric scraps with fusible webbing, place the fabric right side down on ironing surface. Position fusible webbing over the wrong side of fabric. With the protective paper backing on the top, press with high heat setting. When cool, remove the paper backing.

3. Trace the flower and letter shapes, *pages 42–45*, onto tracing paper and cut out. Trace around the pattern pieces onto the fabric. Cut out the pieces neatly with scissors.

4. Arrange the fabric cutouts onto the apron as shown, *left*, and press with iron on high setting. For the flowers, layer different fabrics on top of each other and press without sliding or shifting the material.

5. Using a ⅜-inch-wide flat paintbrush, paint a check pattern onto the apron trim and ties.

apron floral patterns

DRINK THAT MILK

apron lettering patterns

apron flower patterns

EAT THOSE PEAS

apron lettering patterns

last-minute gifts

When you want to remember the special people in your life, there's nothing like a handmade treasure to tell them just how much they mean to you. This chapter is packed with wonderful gifts to make and share with family and friends—even if you have only a few minutes to spare.

Tea Time Napkins and Rings

Tea lovers will adore these boldly striped napkin rings and stamped napkins that display Mary Engelbreit's teapot and teacup motifs.

WHAT YOU'LL NEED FOR THE TAG

Medium-weight papers in light yellow and white
Scissors
Decorative-edged scissors
Glue stick
Round paper punch
Mary Engelbreit® rubber stamp
Black ink pad
Markers in desired colors
Red fine-line marker
¼-inch-wide ribbon

HERE'S HOW

1. Cut a 3¾-inch square from white paper. Cut a 4-inch square from light yellow paper, cutting the last two sides using decorative-edged scissors.
2. Glue the white square atop the yellow. Let the glue dry.
3. With the decorative corner at the top, punch a hole approximately ½ inch from the right corner. Fold the decorative edge down, leaving about ¼ inch of white showing under the decorative edge.
4. Dab the rubber stamp onto the ink pad and stamp the front of the tag. Let the ink dry. Fill in the design as desired using colored markers.
5. Write the desired message inside the tag. Thread the ribbon through the punched hole.

WHAT YOU'LL NEED FOR THE STAMPED NAPKINS AND NAPKIN RINGS

Purchased cloth napkins and iron
Acrylic paints in black and red
Disposable paper plate
Mary Engelbreit's teapot and teacup rubber stamps
Fabric markers in red, yellow, and blue
Purchased wooden napkin rings
½-inch flat paintbrush

HERE'S HOW

1. Iron napkin flat and smooth.
2. Place a small amount of black acrylic paint onto a plate. Spread the paint out thin. Practice stamping with the rubber stamp. Press the stamp into the paint and stamp onto a scrap piece of paper, until you are comfortable with how much paint to use and how much pressure to apply. Stamp randomly on the napkin with the stamp and black paint. Allow the paint to dry.
3. Fill in the areas of the stamped motifs as desired using fabric markers. Allow to dry.
4. Press the napkin with a hot iron.
5. To decorate the napkin rings, paint red stripes onto the rings using red acrylic paint and a ½-inch flat paintbrush. Let the paint dry.

Springtime Garden Hat

All wrapped up in a straw hat—these gardening must-haves are perfect for that special friend with a green thumb.

MORE GIFT-GIVING IDEAS

These garden hats aren't only for gardeners! Use your imagination when selecting what goes in the bonnet. Here are a few ideas:

- For the bird watcher—a bird identifier book, birdseed, and binoculars.
- For the beach lover—sunglasses, sun block lotion, and a beach towel.
- For the home decorator—candles, potpourri, and a floral shop gift certificate.

WHAT YOU'LL NEED

2 yards of red-and-white checked ribbon and scissors
Straw hat
Safety pins, needle, and thread
Silk sunflowers
Garden tools
Sandpaper
Acrylic paints in red, yellow, green, black, and white
Paintbrushes
Garden gloves and floral buttons
Seed packets

HERE'S HOW

1. Cut the ribbon in half. Lay hat down on work surface with crown side up. Lay ribbons on each side of crown, centering them, and fitting snugly around the hat. On each side of the hat, pin the ribbons together where they meet the hat.

2. Using a needle and thread, tack the ribbon to the hat, sewing both sides just enough to hold. Also tack one sunflower head and leaves on top of the ribbon.

3. To paint wooden-handled garden tools, first sand the wooden surface. Paint the base color using red, yellow, or green. Let dry.

4. On the red-handled tool, make black dots. Dip a paintbrush handle in black paint and dot it onto the surface. Let the paint dry. Add a smaller white dot on top of the black dot. If you do not have a tiny enough handle you may use the sharpened end of a pencil dipped in paint.

5. Paint dots on the green-handled tool in the same manner. Paint yellow dots with smaller red dots on top.

6. For the gloves, sew floral buttons onto the cuff area.

7. Place the hat upside-down and lay a bouquet of silk sunflowers in the crown of the hat. Add gardening gloves, the gardening tools, and seed packets. Tie the ribbon ends together firmly to bring the hat brim upward.

Clever Candle Wraps

WHAT YOU'LL NEED FOR THE TAG

Medium-weight papers in red, black, and white
Scissors
Glue stick
Mary Engelbreit® sticker, or motif cut from a card or wrapping paper
Round paper punch
Red fine-line marker
Black cord

HERE'S HOW

1. Cut a 3¼-inch square from red paper. Cut a 3-inch square from black. Cut two 1½-inch squares from white.
2. Glue the black square atop the red. Glue the white squares atop the black, one in the upper left corner, the other in the lower right.
3. Affix the sticker (or glue the cutout motif) in the center of the tag.
4. Punch a hole in the top right corner of the tag.
5. Write the desired messages on the white squares. Thread the cord through the punched hole.

These clever candle "sticks" will make great in-a-hurry gifts or fantastic guest favors for your next gathering!

MORE GIFT-GIVING IDEAS

The presentation is what makes these candles so fun to give and to receive! Any small objects of the same shape will work for this clever "stack-and-wrap" idea:

• Small canned foods or jelly jars
• Rolls of coins
• Sample sizes of shampoo
• Cooking spices

WHAT YOU'LL NEED FOR THE CANDLE WRAPS

4 cylinder-shaped votive candles
Cellophane gift wrap
Scissors
Ribbon in desired colors

HERE'S HOW

1. Stack the votive candles as desired and roll firmly in a piece of cellophane. Wrap the cellophane around the candles at least twice to secure.
2. Twist the ends of cellophane and trim each end evenly to about 3 or 4 inches.
3. Tie the ends closed with several strands of various colored ribbons. Trim the ends.

to Mrs. Blair

from Lizzy

Bon Voyage Bag

Here's the perfect start to an unforgettable vacation—a handy "have- a-good-trip" bag that holds a variety of personalized little necessities.

WHAT YOU'LL NEED

For bag

Stick about 28 inches long

Acrylic paints in yellow, red, blue, purple, green, black, and white

Paintbrushes

Foam plate

15x15-inch piece of fabric

Pinking shears

For accessories

Acrylic enamel paints in black and white

Paintbrush and pencil with a round-tip eraser

Towels, date book, postage stamps, cards, binoculars, or other items for traveling

Hairbrush, comb, toothbrush, or other small accessories

Ribbon

HERE'S HOW

For bag

1. Select a fairly straight and sturdy stick. Scrub it clean and let it dry. Choose as many colors as desired to paint simple patterns on the stick handle. Put a small amount of paint on a plate and use as a palette. Paint colorful rings around the stick. Using a flat paintbrush, paint small square shapes. Dip the handle end of a paintbrush into paint and dot paint onto stick.

2. Trim the piece of fabric using the pinking shears. Lay the fabric flat with the wrong side up. Place gift items in the center and tie two opposite corners once. Place the stick over the knot and tie once more around the stick. Do the same with the two remaining corners.

For accessories

1. Paint simple dots and shapes on the handles of the comb, hairbrush, and toothbrush. To make dots, dip the handle end of a paintbrush in paint and dot onto surface. For larger dots, use a round-tip pencil eraser. Let one side dry thoroughly before turning it over to paint the other side. Let the paint dry.

2. Roll the towels and tie with a ribbon bow.

3. Arrange the accessories in the fabric square and tie onto the stick.

MORE GIFT-GIVING IDEAS

Travelers of all ages will appreciate this clever "sack on a stick." Here are some more ideas of what to pack inside:

- Postcards, stamps, and a camera for an off-to-camp child
- Paperback books and candy for someone going into the hospital
- An address book, stationery, and a pretty pen for a friend who is moving away

A Gift of Good Reading

Give a gift of inspiration that will last all year long—a subscription to a favorite can't-wait-to-read-it magazine.

WHAT YOU'LL NEED FOR THE TAG

Magazine
Medium-weight papers in yellow, red, and white
Pinking shears
Scissors
Glue stick
Round paper punch
¼-inch-wide ribbon
Black fine-line marker

HERE'S HOW

1. Take the magazine to a copy center. Have a reduced color copy made to measure approximately 3x4¼ inches. Trim the excess paper.
2. Cut a ¾x4-inch strip from red paper using pinking shears. Cut a ½x4-inch white strip. Glue the white strip atop the red strip. Glue the strips to the reduced cover at the desired angle. Trim the ends.
3. Glue the cover to a piece of yellow paper, leaving at least ¼ inch of yellow around the edge. Trim the yellow border with pinking shears.
4. Punch a hole in the upper left corner and thread with ribbon. Write desired message on the white strip.

WHAT YOU'LL NEED FOR THE GIFT CERTIFICATE

Sample magazine
Scissors
Glue stick
Colored papers to coordinate with magazine cover
Decorative-edged scissors
Large and small paper punches
Green felt-tip marker
6x9-inch white envelope

HERE'S HOW

1. Make a color copy of the desired magazine cover, reduced to approximately 3x4¼ inches. Cut out the photocopied cover.
2. Glue the cover to a contrasting color paper. Trim around the cover using decorative-edged scissors.
3. Cut the background paper to measure 8½x5½ inches, using the desired scissors. Cut and glue a 2-inch-wide strip of white at the bottom of the certificate as shown, trimming with the same decorative-edged scissors as used for the background paper.
4. Cut a 3½x4½-inch rectangle from a coordinating color of paper. Glue at an angle above white strip as shown. Place the mounted cover over the rectangle.
5. Use paper punches to add dots and flowers as desired. To make leaves, use the large paper punch to cut out large holes. Carefully hold the holes in the punch a second time, trimming off one edge of the hole.
6. To make small swirls, punch small sections off of large punched holes. Glue shapes in place as desired.
7. Write the desired message on the white strip.
8. Use the same techniques to add a decorative band to the front of the envelope.

breit ideas for the holidays

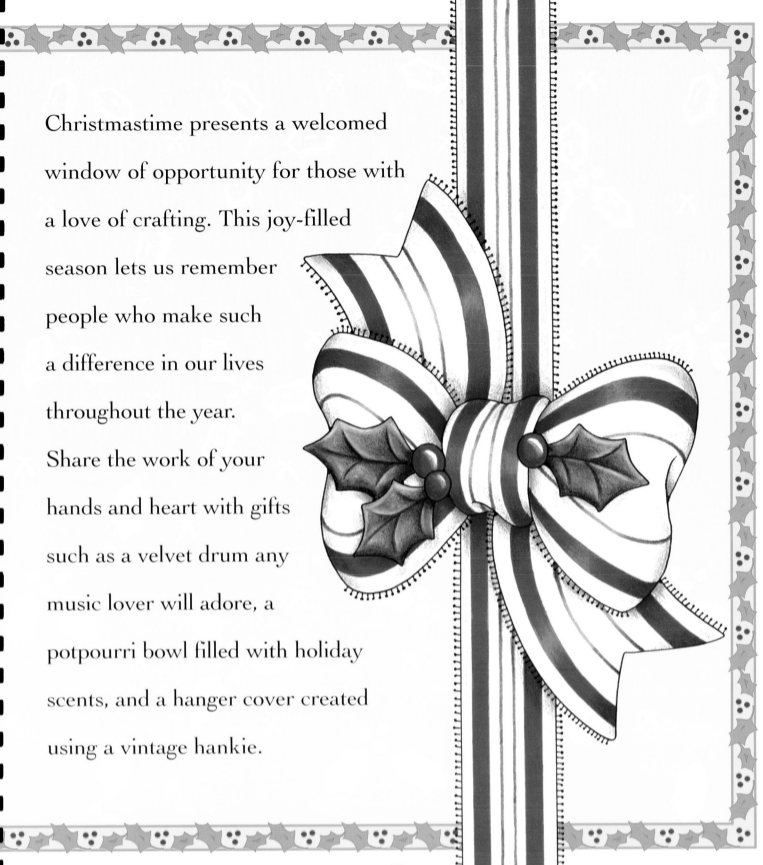

Christmastime presents a welcomed window of opportunity for those with a love of crafting. This joy-filled season lets us remember people who make such a difference in our lives throughout the year. Share the work of your hands and heart with gifts such as a velvet drum any music lover will adore, a potpourri bowl filled with holiday scents, and a hanger cover created using a vintage hankie.

Drum Box

This festive drum box holds gifts of music to be enjoyed year-round.

WHAT YOU'LL NEED FOR THE TAG

Medium-weight papers in black and red
Scissors and pinking shears
Thick white crafts glue
Wooden plug
Acrylic paint in purple and yellow
Paintbrush
Green crafting foam
Paper punch
Cord
Black marker

HERE'S HOW

1. Cut a 4½-inch square from black paper using scissors. Cut a 4-inch square from red using pinking shears. Glue red square atop black.
2. Paint wooden plug purple. Let dry. Add a yellow dot in the center. Let dry. Glue on tag corner.
3. Cut two small green ovals from foam. Glue aside plug as shown.
4. Punch a hole in the opposite corner of flower. Thread cord through hole. Write message in center.

WHAT YOU'LL NEED FOR THE DRUM BOX

Round cardboard box with lid
Pencil
Acrylic paints in white, purple, blue, yellow, and black; paintbrush
Tape measure
Red velvet
Scissors
White cotton fabric
Spray adhesive
Gold braid trim
Thick white crafts glue
String
Straight pins
16 wooden plugs
Green crafting foam or felt
Decorative cording
Dowel and 2 wooden balls with holes

HERE'S HOW

1. Place the lid on box and draw a pencil line where the lid meets.
2. Paint the lid, inside of box, and top portion of outside to the pencil line with white acrylic paint. Let dry.
3. Measure from the pencil line to the bottom, and around the box. Cut red velvet to these measurements.
4. Lay the lid on a piece of white fabric. Trim around the lid, cutting 1¼ inches from the edge.
5. Place lid on box. Spray lid and sides with spray adhesive. Allow the adhesive to dry to a tacky stage. Carefully cover box with the rectangular red piece of red velvet, lining up the bottom edge of fabric with the bottom edge of box.
6. Place the white fabric on a flat surface, with the right side down.

Carefully place the top of the tacky lid onto the center of the fabric. Smooth out the wrinkles and pull the fabric up tightly onto the edges of the lid. Trim off excess fabric.
7. To cover the sides of the lid with gold braid, cut it to the length of the lid circumference. Glue it onto the lid over the white fabric (more than one row of braid may be needed). Glue the same amount of gold trim around the box bottom.
8. To place the plugs onto the drum, cut string the circumference of the box. Divide into 8 portions, and mark the string. Pin onto the red fabric where the pegs will go, and mark the fabric. Do the same on the top portion of the drum along the edge of the red velvet, staggering the marks so that cord can be wound from peg to peg, alternating top to bottom.
9. Paint the plugs a desired color. Let dry. Paint a yellow dot in each center. Cut small oval leaf shapes from green felt or foam. Glue leaves onto the back of the wooden plugs. Glue the painted plugs onto the drum along the edge of the gold braid where marked. Let dry.
10. Wind cord from peg to peg, gluing onto the pegs. (It may help to hold in place with pins until dry.)
11. To make drumsticks, purchase a dowel and round wooden balls with holes that fit snugly onto the end of the dowel. Cut the dowel to a slightly longer length than the diameter of the box lid. Glue the wooden balls onto the dowels. Let dry. Paint the sticks black. Allow to dry. Add white dots by dipping the handle end of a paintbrush in white paint and dotting paint onto the surface. Fill the drum with gift items.

To: Matt
From: Santa

Happy Holiday Jar

WHAT YOU'LL NEED FOR THE TAG

Medium-weight papers in red, green, and white
Scissors
Thick white crafts glue
¾-inch round yellow sticker
¼-inch-wide ribbon
Black fine-line marker

HERE'S HOW

1. Cut a 2-inch circle from red paper. Cut two leaves (one reverse) and three white peppermint stripe shapes using the patterns on *page 110*. Fold the leaves in half lengthwise.
2. Cut a 2-inch circle from white paper. Mark the center of the circle. Divide the circle into six pieces (like on a pie) but instead of drawing straight lines, draw elongated backward "S" lines. Cut out three of these pieces and glue atop the red circle as shown. Affix the yellow sticker in the center.
3. Glue a leaf behind the left and right sides of the circle.
4. Glue ribbons on the back of the circle top. Let the glue dry.
5. Write desired messages on the leaves.

Atop a desk or on the kitchen counter, this jolly jar will get lots of use (and oohs and ahhs) filled with holiday treats.

MORE GIFT-GIVING IDEAS

Painted with holiday colors, this whimsical jar holds candy sticks and so much more. Imagine how pretty it would look with these holiday treasures inside:
• Glass-bead tree garlands
• Cellophane-wrapped popcorn balls
• Christmas cards
• Glitter-covered plastic snowflakes

WHAT YOU'LL NEED FOR THE CANDY JAR

Clear or green tinted glass jar with cork lid
Glass paints in red, white, green, and metallic gold
Paintbrushes
Pencil with round-tip eraser

(continued on pages 64–65)

HERE'S HOW

1. Wash and dry the jar. Avoid touching the areas to be painted.

▼2. To paint flowers, paint various sizes of circles in red or white around the perimeter of the jar. Let the paint dry. To paint the contrasting centers, paint smaller circles. Let the paint dry.

▶3. Use a flat brush to paint green holly leaves where desired, using the photograph for inspiration. Let the paint dry.

▼4. Use a ½-inch flat paintbrush to paint white checks every ½ inch around the base and rim of the jar. Let the paint dry. Paint the alternating checks red. Let the paint dry.

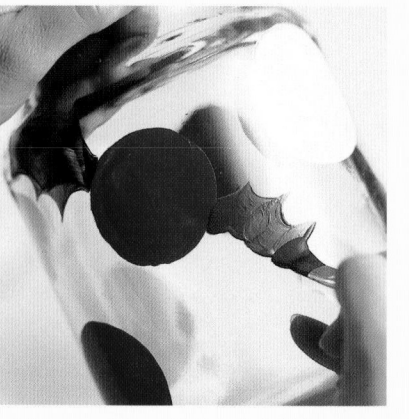

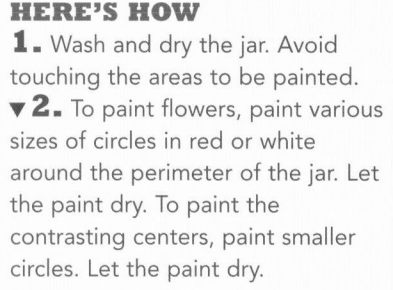

7. Add small gold dots between the leaves and flowers and on the red dots on the rim. Let the paint dry thoroughly. Follow the manufacturer's directions for making the paint permanent.

8. Use the eraser to make green dots on the top of the cork lid. Let the paint dry. Add small white dots on top of and in between the larger green dots. Let dry.

▲ **5.** Use a fine liner brush and gold paint to outline the flower sections and the holly leaves. Add veins to the leaves, if desired.

▶ **6.** Dip the eraser end of a pencil into red paint and dot in the centers of the white checks around the rim. To make small white dots on the red checks, dip the handle end of a small paintbrush into white paint and dot in the center of each red check. Let the paint dry.

Christmas Potpourri

Oh-so-pretty to look at, this painted bowl of potpourri fills the room with holiday scent and Christmas cheer. The bowl can be used for other natural scents after the Christmas season is over.

WHAT YOU'LL NEED FOR THE TAG

Medium-weight papers in white, purple, and yellow
Scissors
Black fine-line marker
Glue stick
Large star paper punch
Round paper punch
¼-inch ribbon

HERE'S HOW

1. Cut a 3-inch circle from white paper. Cut a 2½-inch circle from purple paper.
2. Using a black marker, color in ¼-inch checks around the edge of the white circle (tapering slightly toward the center).
3. Glue the purple circle atop the white circle.
4. Punch out four yellow stars and glue where desired on tag front, leaving center area open for message.
5. Write desired message in center of tag. Punch a round hole in the top of the tag. Thread the ribbon through the hole.

WHAT YOU'LL NEED FOR THE POTPOURRI BOWL

Cedar or pine greenery
Potpourri oil scents
Plastic sandwich bags
Small pinecones
Acrylic paints in black, white, and purple; paintbrush
One Craft Dough Recipe, *right*
Saucepan and stovetop
Red and yellow food coloring
Paper plate or waxed paper
Rolling pin and tiny cookie cutters
Wooden bowl

HERE'S HOW

1. Purchase or gather cedar or pine greenery. They may already have a strong scent and need no added scent. If they do need scent, put a small amount in a plastic sandwich bag, add a few drops of potpourri oil to the bag, shake it thoroughly, and let it sit in enclosed bag for at least an hour.
2. Gather or purchase tiny pine cones. Using a small amount of white acrylic paint, paint them, allowing some of the brown to remain unpainted. Let the paint dry, put them in a small plastic bag, and add a few drops of scent, such as pine or anything else you wish.

3. *Craft Dough Recipe:* To make the dough to cut out shapes, combine 2 cups soda, 1 cup cornstarch, and 1¼ cups water in a saucepan. Place on medium heat, stirring constantly until it begins to bubble and becomes the consistency of mashed potatoes. Remove from heat, cover with cloth, and allow to set until cool enough to handle. Knead it with hands into a smooth clay. Add yellow coloring to half and red to the remaining half. Add scented oils, such as orange or apple spice, if desired.
4. Roll the red dough into small balls, lay on a paper plate or waxed paper, and allow to dry. It may only take an hour. For the yellow stars, roll out the dough, cut out shapes with a cutter, and allow them to dry. If more scent is desired, put the dried dough shapes into a baggie with several drops of scented oil. Shake bag until oil is absorbed, and let sit in bag for about an hour.
5. Paint the entire bowl purple. Let the paint dry. Paint the rim white and let it dry. Paint small black checks onto the white rim. Let the paint dry.
6. Arrange the potpourri and dough shapes in the bowl.

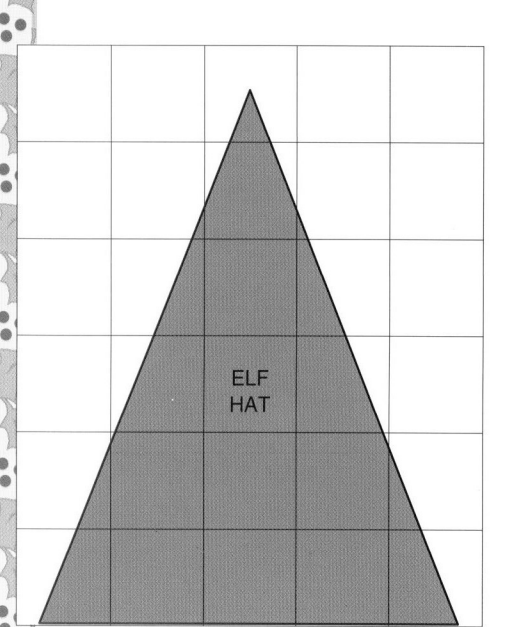

Merry Elf Hats

On the tree or tied to a holiday gift, these tiny felt elf hats, filled with all kinds of goodies, are as merry as can be!

Decorate these mini gift holders with stars, stripes, and polka dots or other desired quick-to-cut motifs.

ELF HAT

1 Square = 1 Inch

WHAT YOU'LL NEED
Tracing paper and pencil
Scissors
Small pieces of felt in red, white,
   black, dark green, spring green,
   turquoise, yellow, purple,
   lavender, and hot pink
Pinking shears
Paper punch
Fusible webbing
Iron
Thick white crafts glue
Yarns in red, green, or other
   desired colors
Needle and thread
Pompons

HERE'S HOW
1. Enlarge and trace the triangle pattern, *left*, onto tracing paper. Cut out and trace onto felt pieces. Cut the backing piece out with regular scissors. Cut the front piece (using pinking shears on the long edges), trimming the sides ⅛ inch. Punch holes in the corners of the backing triangle for hanging.
2. Prepare each cutout shape by applying fusible webbing to the back. Cut a small piece of webbing with paper still attached. Position onto the felt with the paper side up.

Iron webbing onto the felt. The iron should make direct contact with the paper backing only. Use iron on high setting. Allow felt to cool. Peel off paper backing.
3. Cut out desired shapes and thin strips with pinking shears or regular scissors. Punch out dots with a paper punch. When punching holes in felt, it punches out easier if the fused side is up.
4. Arrange all the felt pieces onto the small triangle as desired. Place a piece of paper over the prepared triangle. Iron with a very hot iron, keeping paper still to avoid shifting the small felt pieces.
5. Place small triangle over the large triangle, leaving a border around the two sides. Glue the sides. Let dry until firm. Tie a hanger with yarn looped through the punched holes on the back side of the hat. Sew on a pompon to the tip of the hat. Fill the hats with items such as money, pens and pencils, refrigerator magnets, candy sticks, and other small items.

Vintage Hankie Hanger

Accented with vintage buttons, this covered hanger will be as appreciated as any clothing it accompanies.

WHAT YOU'LL NEED FOR THE TAG

Tracing paper and pencil
Medium-weight papers in black, red, and 1/8-inch black-and-white checkerboard
Scissors and paper punch
Thick white crafts glue
1/4-inch white ribbon with black polka dots
1/8-inch-wide red ribbon
Black marker

HERE'S HOW

1. Trace the hanger pattern, *page 111*, onto tracing paper. Cut out and trace shape on all papers. Cut out the shapes.
2. On the checked paper, cut off the hanger top. On the red paper, cut off the hanger top and 1/4 inch at the bottom. Punch a round hole in the hanger top of the black paper.
3. Glue the checked paper atop the black, aligning the bottoms. Glue the red atop the checked paper, 1/4 inch from bottom edge.
4. Tie a small bow from 1/4-inch ribbon. Trim the ends. Glue the bow just below the punched hole.
5. Thread the 1/8-inch ribbon through the punched hole. Write a message in the center of the tag.

WHAT YOU'LL NEED FOR THE HANGER

Wooden hanger
Acrylic paint
Paintbrush
1/2 yard of black-and-white checked fabric
Fusible interfacing
Vintage holiday handkerchief
Needle and thread
Vintage buttons
Red and green 6mm faceted beads for trim
1/8-inch-wide satin ribbon

HERE'S HOW

1. Paint the hanger in a coordinating or contrasting color as the clothing item, if desired. Let the paint dry.
2. Trace the hanger shape extending the length 1/2 inch. Make a paper pattern of this shape. Fuse the interfacing to the wrong side of the fabric. Trace around the pattern twice on the interfacing. Cut out the two fabric shapes.
3. Trim the corner from a vintage or new handkerchief. Baste it to the hanger cover front using tiny stitches.
4. With right sides facing, stitch the front to the back of the hanger along the sides, leaving several inches open at the top. Clip the seam.
5. Hem the opening at the top and hem along the bottom edge. Add beads to the handkerchief where desired. Sew buttons along the bottom edge. Trim the hanger with a ribbon bow.

gifts of goodies

Everyone appreciates a tasty surprise no matter what the occasion. Find out how easy it is to capture a snowflake impression on a mug (and don't forget to fill it with yummy hot chocolate mix). Or, transform a gourd into a bowl that's truly a work of art. What makes each of these containers so unique is that they'll "keep" long after the goodies are gone.

Snowflake Etched Mug

WHAT YOU'LL NEED FOR THE TAG

Medium-weight purple paper
Scissors
Decorative-edged scissors
Round paper punch
White enamel paint
Fine-liner paintbrush
1-inch-wide sheer white ribbon

HERE'S HOW

1. Cut a 2¼x4-inch rectangle from purple paper using the straight-edged scissors. Use the decorative-edged scissors to cut the right end to a point, starting approximately 2½ inches from the left edge. Punch a hole opposite the point.
2. Paint a border on the tag as desired. Add a snowflake to the point by painting three ½-inch-long intersecting lines. Add snowflake details by painting small "Vs," lines, and dots on or by the intersecting lines. Write the desired message in the center. Let the paint dry.
3. Thread the ribbon through the hole.

Captured on glass to enjoy all winter long, this etched snowflake design can also be used to decorate coordinating glass plates.

MORE GIFT-GIVING IDEAS

Hot chocolate makes a great "stuffer" for this elegantly etched mug. Other cold-weather ideas include:
• Packaged flavored coffees
• Select tea packets
• Cinnamon sticks and hot cider mix
• Peppermint sticks
• Red and green candies
• A wrapped stack of homemade snowflake-frosted sugar cookies

WHAT YOU'LL NEED FOR THE MUG

Contact paper or 3-inch-long labels
Pinking shears and scissors
Self-adhesive reinforcements
Masking tape
Rubber gloves
Paintbrush
Etching cream

(continued on pages 76–77)

HERE'S HOW

▼ **1.** Cut two 2-inch-long narrow strips from Contact paper or label using a pinking shears. (Practice cutting so the strip forms a continuous line of diamond shapes.) Cut two 1½-inch-long straight strips, approximately 1⁄16 inch wide. Cut eight ¼-inch-long pieces that are approximately 1⁄16 inch wide.

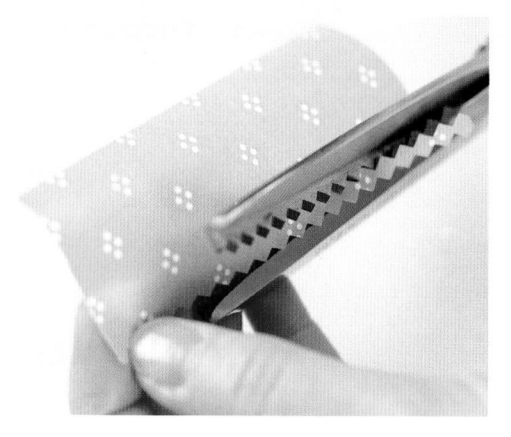

2. Peel the backing off, and place the diamond strips in a "plus" formation on the front of the mug. Place the narrow strips between the diamond-shaped strips.

◀ **3.** Place a reinforcement on the end of each strip.

▼ **4.** Place the short strips in "V" formations in the center of each long narrow strip.

5. Place a row of reinforcements around the base of the mug. Make sure each piece is pressed firmly into place.

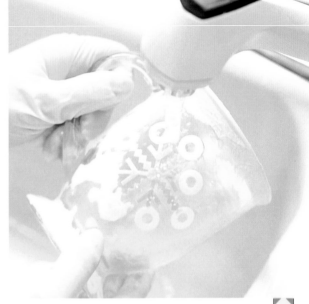

▲ **6.** Press a length of masking tape around the top edge of the mug, covering about ¼ inch.

▶ **7.** Put on rubber gloves. Use a paintbrush to cover the mug with etching cream. Follow the manufacturer's directions for etching the glass and washing the cream away.

▲ **8.** Wearing rubber gloves, remove all of the stickers and wash the mug thoroughly in hot soapy water. Rinse and repeat.

Dandy Sandy Boxes

These unique boxes, embellished with sand and colorful paint, are as much fun to make as they are to give.

WHAT YOU'LL NEED FOR THE TAG

Tracing paper
Pencil
Old scissors
Sandpaper
Acrylic paints in purple and black
Paintbrush
Paper punch
Thick white crafts glue
White paint pen
¼-inch-wide ribbon

HERE'S HOW

1. Trace the smaller heart pattern, *page 110*, onto a piece of tracing paper. Cut out shape. Trace around shape on sandpaper. Cut out. Cut a 3x3-inch square from sandpaper.
2. Paint the smooth side of the square black. Let dry. Paint the rough side black. Let dry. Punch a hole in one corner, approximately ¼ inch from the edges. Paint the rough side of the heart shape purple. Let dry.
3. With the punched hole at the top and the rough sides up, glue the heart shape in the center of the square. Let dry.
4. Using white paint pen, outline the heart shape and add dots to the black area. Write desired message in the heart. Let dry. Thread ribbon through hole at top.

MORE GIFT-GIVING IDEAS

Great for all ages, this sand-covered heart box can house a variety of treats. Select the size heart box you desire, then fill it with small bags of any of these much-appreciated snacks:
- Flavored popcorn
- Candy-dipped pretzels
- Petit fours
- Trail mix
- Cookies
- Wrapped candies
- Nuts
- Fresh fruit
- Mints
- Cereal snack mix

WHAT YOU'LL NEED FOR THE BOX

Paper to cover work surface
Pencil
Cardboard box in any shape and size
Mod Podge decoupage medium
Sand
Acrylic paints in yellow, orange, blue, turquoise, dark green, lime green, red, pink, purple, lavender, black, and white; flat paintbrush
Tracing paper and scissors
White paint pen
Cellophane bags or wrap

(continued on pages 80–81)

HERE'S HOW

▼ **1.** Cover work surface with paper. With lid securely on, draw a line where lid meets box.

▶ **2.** Coat the entire outside surface with an even and generous coat of decoupage medium. Avoid getting glue on the area on the base where the lid will sit.

▼ **3.** Cover the glue with sand. Pour it onto the decoupage medium, tap off the extra sand and repeat this process until the box is covered. Let dry and coat the entire piece with another coat of decoupage medium. Allow it to dry.

▲ **4.** You can leave a natural sand-colored background or paint it using desired colors of paint. If using paint, use a flat brush. The surface will take a lot of paint.

▲ **5.** To add shapes, draw desired shapes on tracing paper and cut out. Trace around designs (we've used hearts) as many times as desired on the box. To make the color shaded, paint the shape solid first. Allow the paint to dry. Then using very little paint on the brush, lightly brush one end of the shape with a lighter shade of the same or similar color. Put more paint on one side and fade it off about halfway across the shape. For the colors used on this box, use a dark blue base highlighted with turquoise, dark purple with lavender, dark red with pink, orange with yellow, and dark green with lime green. After the paint is dry, outline the shapes and add desired details with a white paint pen.

6. Line the box with cellophane or place goodies into bags before placing into box.

Salad Lover's Salad Set

MORE GIFT-GIVING IDEAS

This cheery set is filled with tasty surprises for salad lovers—plus a painted salad fork and spoon—but could be filled with other food items as well. Here are some optional food ideas to delight that special someone on your gift list:

- Spaghetti, sauce, Parmesan cheese, and breadsticks
- Chili mix, beans, sauce, and oyster crackers
- Fresh pineapple, oranges, apples, and bananas
- Muffin mix, paper muffin cups, and a pair of hot pads
- Vegetable seeds for the garden
- Taco mix, flour shells, corn chips, nacho cheese, and salsa

With a few simple painting techniques, you can create a festive salad set to give to friends who enjoy fresh-from-the-garden bounty.

WHAT YOU'LL NEED

Clear salad bowl
Glass paints suitable for use on eating utensils in grass green, lettuce green, yellow, orange, and magenta; paintbrush
Wooden salad utensils
Acrylic paints in yellow, orange, lime green, magenta, and grass green
Light green tissue paper
Suggested gift items: packaged gourmet salad dressings, seasoned vinegar, gourmet olives, croutons, bacon bits, tomatoes, peppers, and herbs

HERE'S HOW

1. Wash and dry the salad bowl thoroughly. Avoid touching areas of the bowl that will be painted.
2. Painting only on the outside of the bowl, paint a wide band of yellow around the top. Add lines and stripes as shown using a narrow flat brush. Make random squares using a flat brush and one short smooth stroke with plenty of paint. Make dots by dipping the handle end of a paintbrush in paint and dotting it onto surface. Let paint dry for 24 hours. Bake in oven if instructed by the paint manufacturer.
3. Paint the wooden utensil handles with acrylic paints using the same techniques as for the bowl. Paint stripes, lines, and dots. Let the paint dry between coats.
4. After all painting is done, lay light green tissue paper into the bowl. Arrange the items, putting in the utensils first, then the bottles, and the perishable items on top.

Graduation Hat for a Star

MORE GIFT-GIVING IDEAS

Hats off to the graduate! This painted box is just the right size for holding celebration cookies and other goodies, too.

Here are some other "fillers" that high school graduates will surely appreciate:

- Soap, shampoo, toothpaste, and other dorm-room toiletries
- Pens, pencils, notebooks, and a pocket dictionary
- Rolls of quarters to do laundry, and fabric softener sheets

While graduation caps may be happily tossed into the air, this one will rest beautifully on a table, filled with goodies and best wishes for a successful future.

WHAT YOU'LL NEED

Acrylic paints in yellow, pastel green, very light pastel green, white, black, red, lavender, and peach; paintbrush
13½-inch-square piece of cardboard
Pencil
Ruler
Fun foam in any color for stamp
Thick white crafts glue
Circle template

Permanent black fine-point marker
Crafts knife
Button
Purchased tassel
Cord or embroidery floss, optional
Round box with lid about 9¼ inches in diameter
Rubber band
Clear water-based varnish

(continued on page 86)

Congratulations!

HERE'S HOW

1. Paint one side of the cardboard square a solid pastel green. Paint the other side white.

2. On the white side, use a pencil and ruler to lightly draw lines for the borders, marking the line for the green border 1¼ inches in from all the edges. Draw another line ½ inch inside the first lines. Make light pencil marks every ½ inch in the white border, indicating where the checks will be painted. Paint the black checks with a flat ⅜-inch-wide brush. Let the paint dry.

3. Paint the light green border, covering any imperfections from the checks. Let the paint dry. Paint the inside square yellow. Apply a second coat of paint, if needed. Let the paint dry.

◄**4.** To make a small leaf stamp, cut a tiny leaf shape from the sheet of crafting foam and glue it onto a flat end of a pencil. Using your handmade stamp, dip it in pale green paint and stamp the leaf pattern onto the green border. Let the paint dry.

▲**5.** Draw flowers using a circle template. Paint the flowers red, lavender, and peach. To make the yellow dot centers, dip the end of a paintbrush handle or pencil eraser in yellow paint and dot onto the center of each flower. Add green leaves by painting oblong oval shapes. Paint white dots on the yellow area, using the same dotting technique. Let the paint dry.

6. Outline the flowers and the leaves with a fine-point black permanent marker. Write and then paint "Congratulations!" in your own handwriting.

▼ **7.** Find the center of the lid, pierce it with a crafts knife, and cut a little piece out just deep enough to position the button. Using a generous amount of glue, affix the button onto the pierced indented center. Let the glue dry.

8. Slip the tassel loop over the button. If the tassel loop is not long enough to hang over the edge of the square, extend it with embroidery floss or cord in the same color.
▶ **9.** Paint the edges and the underside of the lid. Let the paint dry. Glue the top side of the lid to the center of the underside of the square. Let the glue dry.

▶ **10.** Paint the inside of the container lavender. Let the paint dry. On the outside, measure 1¾ inches from the bottom, marking this measurement every few inches. Place a rubber band around the container 1¾ inches from the bottom, using the marks as a guide. Draw a pencil line next to the rubber band. Remove the rubber band.
11. Paint the top portion of the container yellow. Paint flowers in the same manner as on the lid. Add white dots and outline the flowers. Let the paint dry.

12. Finish with a coat of varnish.

Gourd Nut Bowl

Using some of nature's most intriguing finds, this gourd bowl is trimmed with a band of acorn caps and gourd seeds and filled with a mound of nuts in their own natural shells.

WHAT YOU'LL NEED FOR THE TAG

Medium-weight ivory paper
Scissors
4x4-inch piece of brown kraft paper
Thick white crafts glue
Round paper punch
Acorn cap
Gourd seeds
Ivory acrylic paint
Paintbrush
Black fine-line marker
Heavy jute

HERE'S HOW

1. Cut a 3½-inch square from ivory paper. Fold edges of kraft paper to make a 3-inch square, creasing folds. Carefully tear paper along folds.
2. Glue brown square atop ivory. Use a paper punch to make a hole in corner. In the opposite corner, glue an acorn cap and four gourd seeds as shown. Paint the center of the acorn cap ivory. Let dry.
3. Write desired message on tag. Thread the jute through hole.

WHAT YOU'LL NEED FOR THE BOWL

Round gourd with flat bottom
Pencil
Handsaw
Gourd seeds
Soapy water
Scrubber
Wood stain
Sponge for staining
Cream-colored acrylic paint
Paintbrush
Acorn caps
Thick white crafts glue
Clear varnish
Jute in thick and thin widths
Raffia

HERE'S HOW

1. Draw a pencil line around the gourd where the top will be cut off. Using a handsaw, carefully cut along the drawn line.
2. Clean out the inside of the gourd, saving the seeds to use as decoration on the bowl. Clean the outside of the gourd. Scrub off the outer layer of skin, using soapy water and a steel scrubber. Use the edge of a sharp knife if necessary. Let the gourd dry thoroughly.
3. Apply a wood stain to the outside surface, as if staining wood. Rub this in and let it dry.
4. Draw a pencil line about 1 inch from the top edge. Paint this border area cream. Let it dry.
5. Stain the acorn caps and gourd seeds with wood stain, rub off excess stain, and allow them to dry. Paint a small cream dot in the center of each acorn cap. Apply a generous amount of glue to the back side of the acorn caps and glue onto the painted area. Allow the glue to dry.
6. Glue gourd seeds around the acorn caps for leaves. Coat the entire gourd inside and out with a clear coat of varnish. Coat the inside of the gourd with two or three coats.
7. Glue jute around the bowl as shown. Fill with nuts and add a nutcracker tied in raffia.

To Dad Love, Lori & Bob

presents for the children

Better get ready...these fun gift ideas are going to bring great big snugly bear hugs! Imagine a colorful mini wagon (just a toddler's size) to tote favorite toys of all kinds. And what little princess wouldn't love a phone of her own, brightly painted and trimmed with gems? Whether your little one likes to play cards or build snowmen, some adorable projects await.

Queen's Phone

Treat your little princess regally by making this glamorous phone and presenting it to her in a bright bag trimmed with crown jewels.

WHAT YOU'LL NEED FOR THE TAG

Medium-weight papers in red and yellow
Decorative-edged scissors
Thick white crafts glue
Mary Engelbreit® sticker
Round paper punch
Triangular gem
Gold paint pen
Red fine-line marker
¼-inch-wide ribbon

HERE'S HOW

1. Cut a 2¾-inch square from red paper. Cut a 1½x2¾-inch piece from yellow. Turning the red piece as a diamond shape, glue the yellow piece across the center.
2. Affix the sticker on the bottom of the tag as shown. Punch a hole in the top corner.
3. Center and glue a gem at the top of the yellow paper. Let the glue dry. Outline the gem using gold paint pen. Let the paint dry.
4. Write the desired message on the yellow paper. Thread the ribbon through the punched hole.

phone bag crown pattern

WHAT YOU'LL NEED FOR THE PHONE

Telephone
Acrylic paints in purple, lavender, red, and yellow; paintbrush
Mary Engelbreit's® It's Good to Be Queen greeting card
Scissors
Mod Podge decoupage medium
Clear varnish
Ribbon, optional
Thick white crafts glue
Heart-shaped jewels
Black cording

HERE'S HOW

1. Paint the bottom phone section lavender. Using the photograph, *right*, paint the remaining sections as desired. Let dry. Add vertical stripes to bottom using a ¼-inch flat brush and lavender paint. Let dry.
2. Cut out motif from greeting card or other item that is to be decoupaged on the receiver. Apply a coat of decoupage medium to the back of the cutout and affix onto the phone. Let dry. Coat the phone receiver top with another coat of decoupage medium.
3. Paint two coats of clear varnish over the painted areas, allowing to dry between coats. Be careful not to let varnish seep inside the phone.

4. Glue a band of ribbon around the phone if desired. Glue heart-shaped jewels on and around ribbon, jewels on the receiver, and black cording where there are color divisions.

WHAT YOU'LL NEED FOR THE PHONE BAG

14x12-inch piece of sheer red fabric
Scissors
Sewing machine and matching thread
Tracing paper
Pencil
Scrap of yellow felt
Rhinestones
Thick white crafts glue
Purple ribbon

HERE'S HOW

1. If necessary, adjust the size of the sheer fabric to fit phone.
2. Fold fabric in half. Sew the side and bottom seams. Fold the top edge down and sew a 2-inch hem. Turn inside out and press.
3. Trace the crown shape, *left*, onto tracing paper. Cut out and trace onto yellow felt. Cut out as many crowns as desired and glue randomly onto the bag. Glue rhinestones at each point.
4. Tie the bag with a generous length of purple ribbon.

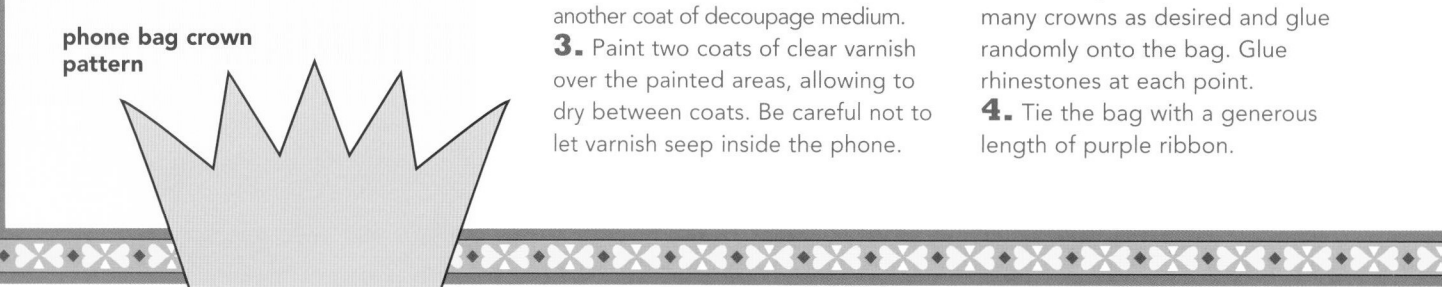

Fun·Wheelin' Wagons

MORE GIFT-GIVING IDEAS

These wagons are just the right size for almost any toy. Paint an even smaller version (10 inches or less) for other tiny treasures for kids, including:

- Jewelry
- Music CDs
- Personalized pens and pencils
- Beads and other crafts supplies
- A camera and film
- Stationery and stamps

Paint these wagons with dots and checks using enamel paints, and with a little imagination, they're ready to roll! Fill with toys and goodies of all sorts.

WHAT YOU'LL NEED

Small wagon
White spray primer and desired color of spray enamel paint for base, if desired
Enamel paints in desired colors
Paintbrush
Pencil with round-tip eraser

HERE'S HOW

1. If the wagon is disassembled, paint the pieces before assembly.

If the wagon is purchased assembled, tape off any areas where the original base paint color is desired.

2. To change the base coat color, first spray with white primer and let dry. Spray the desired area of wagon with enamel. Let the paint dry. Use spray paint to change the color of the wheels and caps, if desired.

3. Use a brush and bottled enamel paints to add stripes, circular flowers and leaves, and checks and squares to wagon. To make polka dots, dip the eraser end of a pencil into paint and dot it on the surface. Let all paint dry thoroughly.

4. If the wagon is disassembled, assemble it according to the manufacturer's instructions. Fill with toys, crayons, books, or other goodies.

Playing Card Box

It's fun to play cards, especially when you keep your decks in a clever box that's labeled with all your favorite games!

WHAT YOU'LL NEED FOR THE TAG

Tracing paper, pencil, and scissors
Decorative-edged scissors
Medium-weight papers in black and lavender
White perforated paper
Glue stick
White acrylic paint and paintbrush
Paper punch
¼-inch-wide ribbon and black marker

HERE'S HOW

1. Trace spade pattern, *page 111.* and cut out. Trace around pattern on black paper. Cut out.
2. Cut a 6½x3½-inch piece from black paper using decorative-edged scissors. Fold in half. Cut a 3x3¼-inch piece from perforated paper and glue to front of tag. Cut two 2¾x3-inch pieces from lavender. Glue one atop the perforated paper and the other inside. Glue spade on the tag front.
3. To add white dots to the spade, dip the handle end of a paintbrush into paint and dab on the surface. Let the paint dry.
4. Punch a hole in the tag corner. Thread ribbon through hole. Write desired message on tag.

WHAT YOU'LL NEED FOR THE CARD BOX

Wood playing card box
Metallic water-based paints in emerald green, purple, pearl white, and dark pink
Paintbrush
Alphabet macaroni
Thick white crafts glue
Four 1-inch-high wooden flower pots
½-inch wooden ball knob
Two 1-inch decorative hinges
Liquid Nails adhesive for woodworking
Black fine-tip permanent marker

HERE'S HOW

1. Paint lid of box with emerald green paint. Paint the bottom with pearl white. Let the paint dry.
2. Using the photo as a guide, decide which card game titles you wish to spell out on the lid of the box. Find all of the macaroni letters needed to spell out each of the titles. Glue the card game titles to the lid where desired. Let the glue dry.

3. Paint vertical purple stripes around the outside of the base. Dip the tip of the paintbrush in pink paint to add dots on the white stripes. Let the paint dry.
4. Paint pink and purple hearts, diamonds, clubs, and spades between the words on the box lid. Add white dots to the lid top and sides. Let the paint dry.
5. Highlight the words by brushing each with a light coat of pearl white paint. Let the paint dry.
6. Paint the flower pots and the knob with pink paint. Let the paint dry. Using adhesive, glue the flower pots, top side up, to the four corners of the box bottom approximately ¼ inch in from the edges. Adhere the knob to the center of the front side of the lid. Let the adhesive dry.
7. Outline the shapes as desired using a permanent black marker.
8. Place the lid on the bottom, aligning the sides. Glue the hinges on the back side, each about ½ inch in from the edge.

Sam the Snowman Kit

To: Emma & Ryan From: Aunt Sue

WHAT YOU'LL NEED FOR THE TAG
Pencil
Medium-weight papers in white, green, yellow, orange, black, and red
Scissors
Pinking shears
Paper punch
Glue stick
Cording
Black fine-line marker

HERE'S HOW
1. Draw and cut a 2- and a 3-inch circle from white paper. Cut a 1x6-inch wide strip from red. Cut a ¼x3-inch strip from red using pinking shears. Cut a green triangle that is 2½ inches at the bottom for the hat. Cut a dime-size circle for pompon using pinking shears. Cut a small orange triangle for nose. Cut a half circle from black for mouth. Use a paper punch to cut two black eyes and four yellow dots for hat.
2. Cut "V" notches in the ends of the 1-inch-wide red strip. Cut it in half. Glue to the top of the larger white circle as shown, *above*. Glue the smaller white circle on the scarf.
3. Glue the hat and facial features in place. Punch a hole in pompon and thread cording through for tie. Write desired message on the tag.

WHAT YOU'LL NEED FOR THE SNOWMAN KIT
Styrofoam cone about 3x5 inches
Sharp knife
Acrylic paint in orange and black
Paintbrush
Wooden clothespins
Liquid Nails weatherproof adhesive
Tracing paper and pencil
Scissors and pinking shears
¼-inch thick crafting foam in purple, blue, yellow, pink, and green
Scarf and black top hat (available in crafts and costume shops)

HERE'S HOW
1. To make the snowman's nose, use a 3x5-inch Styrofoam cone. To shape the cone to look like a carrot, shave a little from the edges, particularly at the base, to make it narrower. Then firmly squeeze and roll the cone to compact the

Pull a snowman out of a hat with this enchanting gift. Anyone with a yard full of snow will know how to work the magic.

Styrofoam. This will make it more solid, eliminate some crumbs, and it will help the Styrofoam to take paint more easily. Paint the nose orange. Allow the paint to dry.
2. Press a clothespin into the center of the Styrofoam nose about 1 inch. Remove it momentarily and squeeze enough weatherproof adhesive into the hole to hold in place. Insert the pin. Let the adhesive dry.
3. To make the eyes, mouth, and buttons, trace the shapes, *page 101*, onto tracing paper, cut them out, and trace onto crafting foam. Cut out the shapes. You may use pinking shears to cut the flower centers.
4. Glue the flower pieces together using weatherproof adhesive. Cut out the eyes, mouth, and flowers. Cut two crosswise slits in the center of each object. Paint the ends of the clothespins black. Let dry. Insert the clothespins in the slits.
5. To assemble as a gift, lay the scarf flat. Place the pieces in the center and tie up in a bundle, making the scarf into a bow. Place the bundle into the snowman hat.

sam the snowman pieces

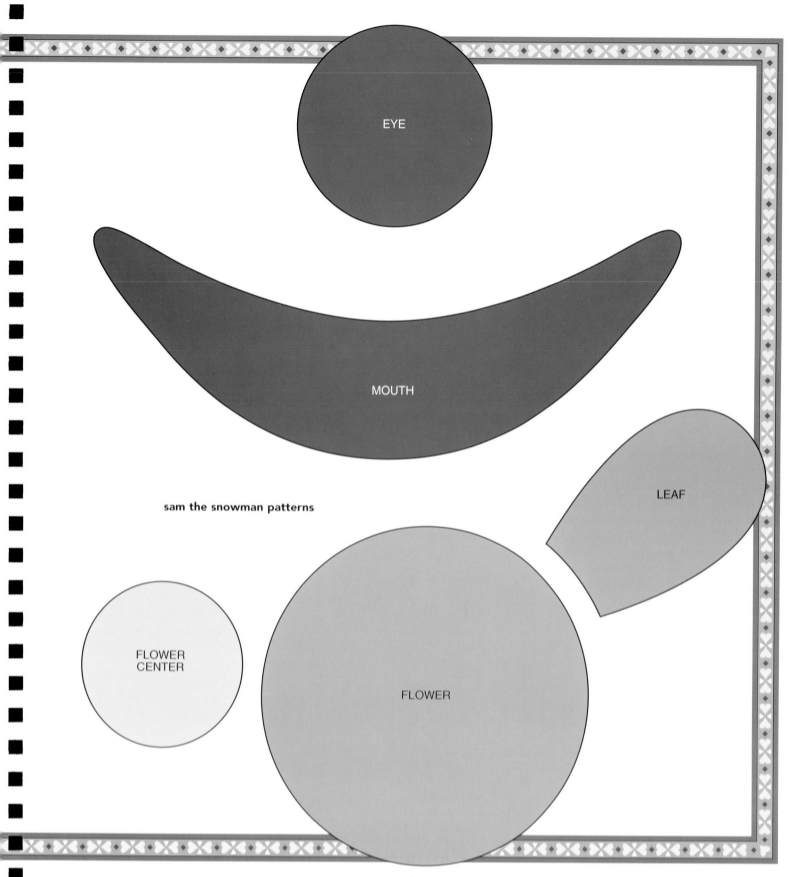

EYE

MOUTH

LEAF

sam the snowman patterns

FLOWER
CENTER

FLOWER

Good-Luck Game Bag

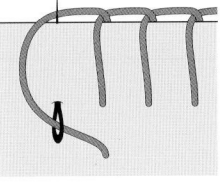

With shoelaces for ties and buttons for trim, this felt game bag will please any game-playing boy or girl.

WHAT YOU'LL NEED FOR THE TAG

Medium-weight yellow paper
Scissors
Paper punch
2¾x2¾-inch piece of red felt
2¼x2¼-inch piece of yellow felt
Needle
Black, red, and yellow embroidery floss
¾-inch green button
½-inch blue button
Black bead
Thick white crafts glue
Tape
Black marker

HERE'S HOW

1. Cut a 3x8-inch piece from yellow paper. Fold the paper in half, short edges together.
2. Use paper punch to make two holes (through both thicknesses) near fold, approximately ½ inch apart.
3. Place the yellow felt square in the center of the red square. Sew together using blanket stitches.
4. Sew the buttons and bead in the center of the yellow felt square.
5. Glue the felt squares in the center of tag front. Let dry.
6. Cut two 14-inch lengths of each floss color. Align one end of each length and knot. Tape the knotted end to a work surface and braid the three flosses. Knot the opposite end. Thread through holes in tag.
7. Write desired message at the bottom and on the inside of the tag.

WHAT YOU'LL NEED FOR THE BAG

12x12-inch piece of red felt
Eyelets and eyelet tool
Two 19-inch dance shoe laces
Two 2-inch squares of yellow felt
Scissors
Black and other desired colors of embroidery floss
Needle
A variety of buttons
Four black beads
Two large white buttons
Marbles, jacks, dominoes, or other small game pieces

HERE'S HOW

1. Draw a 10-inch diameter circle in the center of the red felt (some ice-cream bucket lids are this size). Use the eyelet tool to place eyelets around the circle with the finished side of the eyelet on the undrawn side of the felt. Place two eyelets ¼ inch apart, leaving a 1½-inch space between pairs.
2. Tie the ends of the shoe laces together. With the knot on the inside of the bag, thread the ends of the laces through the eyelets until the ends meet at a pair of eyelets.
3. Cut the yellow felt squares in half diagonally. Use a blanket stitch, *below*, to sew a yellow triangle to the wrong side of each corner of the red felt square, leaving about ¼ inch of red showing at the edge. Fold each of the corners over the right side of the eyelets, tacking the corner with a button and black bead.
4. Sew buttons around the bag as desired, below the drawstring. Lace the shoestring ends through the holes in the large white buttons. Fill the bag with the desired game pieces, and tie the drawstring into a bow.

blanket stitch

fun-to-make bows

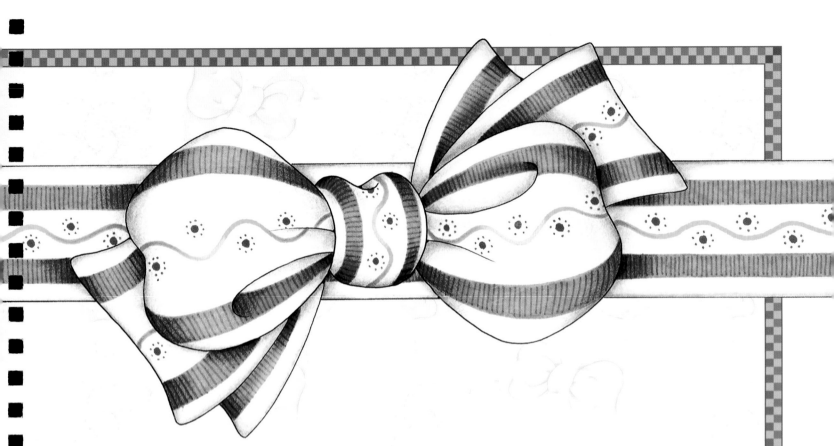

Make the wrap as grand as the gift itself with these
whimsical, fun-to-make bows. Made from supplies you
probably have on hand, these trims are so quick to whip
up, you can make them by the dozens to tuck away for
extra-special gift toppers.

Fun and Fancy Bows

These clever bows are the grand finale for handcrafted gifts you make and give with love. Use your imagination (as well as your leftover crafting supplies) to make all your package toppers ever so "breit."

FELT BOW

WHAT YOU'LL NEED
Tracing paper and pencil
7x6-inch pieces of red, black, and white felts
8x1½-inch piece of red felt
Pinking shears
Mary Engelbreit® pin for center

HERE'S HOW
1. Trace the bow patterns, *page 108*, onto tracing paper.
Using pinking shears, cut the large bow from the red felt, the medium bow from the black felt, and the small bow from the white. Trim the remaining piece of red felt using pinking shears.
2. Place the bow shapes atop each other, with the white bow on top and the red on the bottom. Tie the red felt strip around the bows, leaving the tails on the back side of the bow. Attach the pin to the center of the bow.

WOODEN FLORAL BOW

WHAT YOU'LL NEED
One 1-inch-wide tongue depressor
Acrylic paints in medium green, white, yellow-orange, and black
Paintbrush
Pencil with round-tip eraser
2½-inch diameter wooden circle
Seven 1-inch-long wooden petal shapes
1 miniature wooden apple
Thick white crafts glue

HERE'S HOW
1. Cut the ends off the tongue depressor and paint it black. Paint the wooden circle green, the petals white, and the apple yellow-orange. Let dry.
2. Glue the petals in the center of the green circle. Glue the yellow apple in the center of the petals. Glue the circle in the center of the tongue depressor.
3. Add polka dots around the flower by dipping the handle end of the paintbrush into white paint and dotting on the surface. Add large white dots on the black using a round-tip pencil eraser. Let the paint dry.

STICKER BOW

WHAT YOU'LL NEED
Tracing paper and pencil
12x4-inch piece of light blue
 paper
Scissors and stapler
Mary Engelbreit® stickers

HERE'S HOW
1. Trace the bow pattern, *page 108*,
onto tracing paper. Transfer the pattern
to the blue paper and cut out the shape.
2. Overlap the ends and bring to the center of
the bow shape. Staple the ends in place.
3. Cover the staples with a large sticker. Use small stickers
to decorate each side of the bow as desired.

PAPER STAR BOW

WHAT YOU'LL NEED
Tracing paper and pencil
7x7-inch piece of yellow paper; 6x6-inch piece of blue paper
Scissors
Star paper punch
Glue stick

HERE'S HOW
1. Trace the bow patterns, *page 109*, onto tracing paper.
Transfer the large bow pattern to the yellow paper
and the small bow to the blue paper. Cut out the bow shapes.
2. Use the paper punch to make stars on the blue bow.
 Glue the blue bow atop the yellow in the center.
 3. Gently bend
 the blue bow
 to give it
 dimension.

BEADED BOW

WHAT YOU'LL NEED
18-inch-long piece of black crafts wire
32 large black beads
32 white pony beads
One large red wood bead

HERE'S HOW
1. Tie a knot in one end of
the wire. Alternating colors,
thread on seven black beads and
six white. Thread the red bead onto
the wire.
2. Starting with white, thread on ten
white beads and nine black,
alternating colors as the beads are
placed on the wire. Push the end of
the wire through the red bead.
3. Repeat Step 2.
4. Alternating colors, thread on
seven black beads and six white. Knot
the end of the wire close to the
beads. Trim the remaining wire.

BUTTON BOW

WHAT YOU'LL NEED
Needle and red thread
One ⅞-inch pink button
One 1½-inch yellow button
Three ⅞-inch green buttons
1-inch-wide ribbon

HERE'S HOW
1. Sew the pink button
atop the yellow button.
2. Glue the two green
buttons on the back edge of
the yellow button. Glue the
remaining green button
opposite the pair. Let the
glue dry. Glue bow onto ribbon.

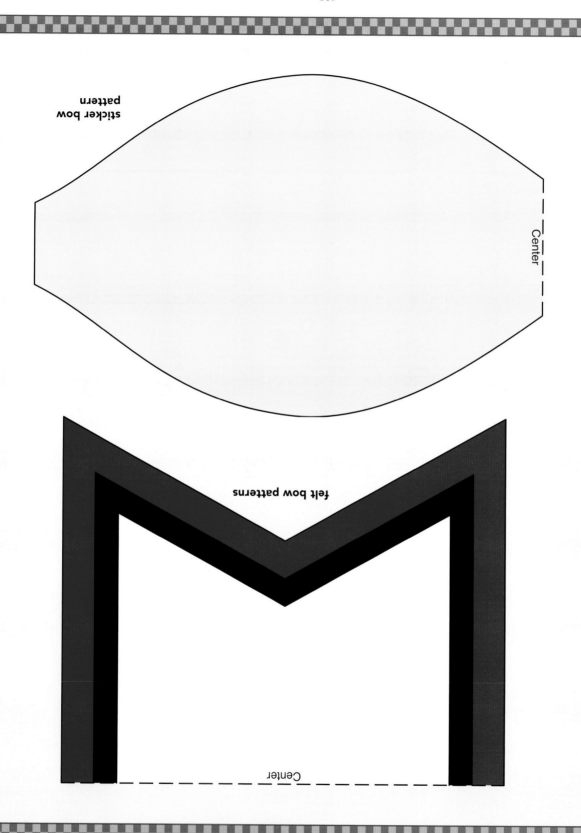

sticker bow pattern

Center

felt bow patterns

Center

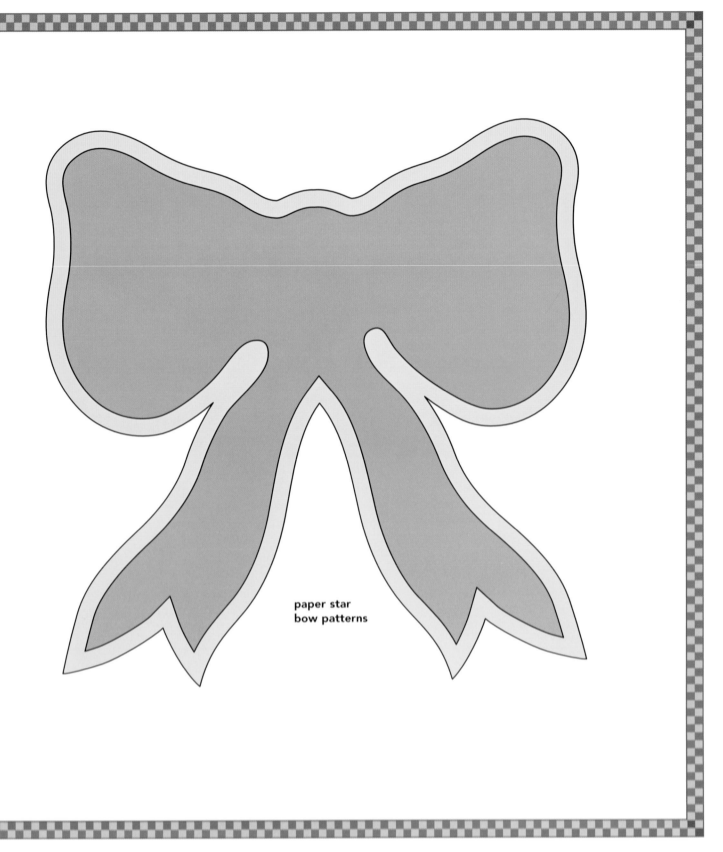

paper star
bow patterns

Tag Patterns

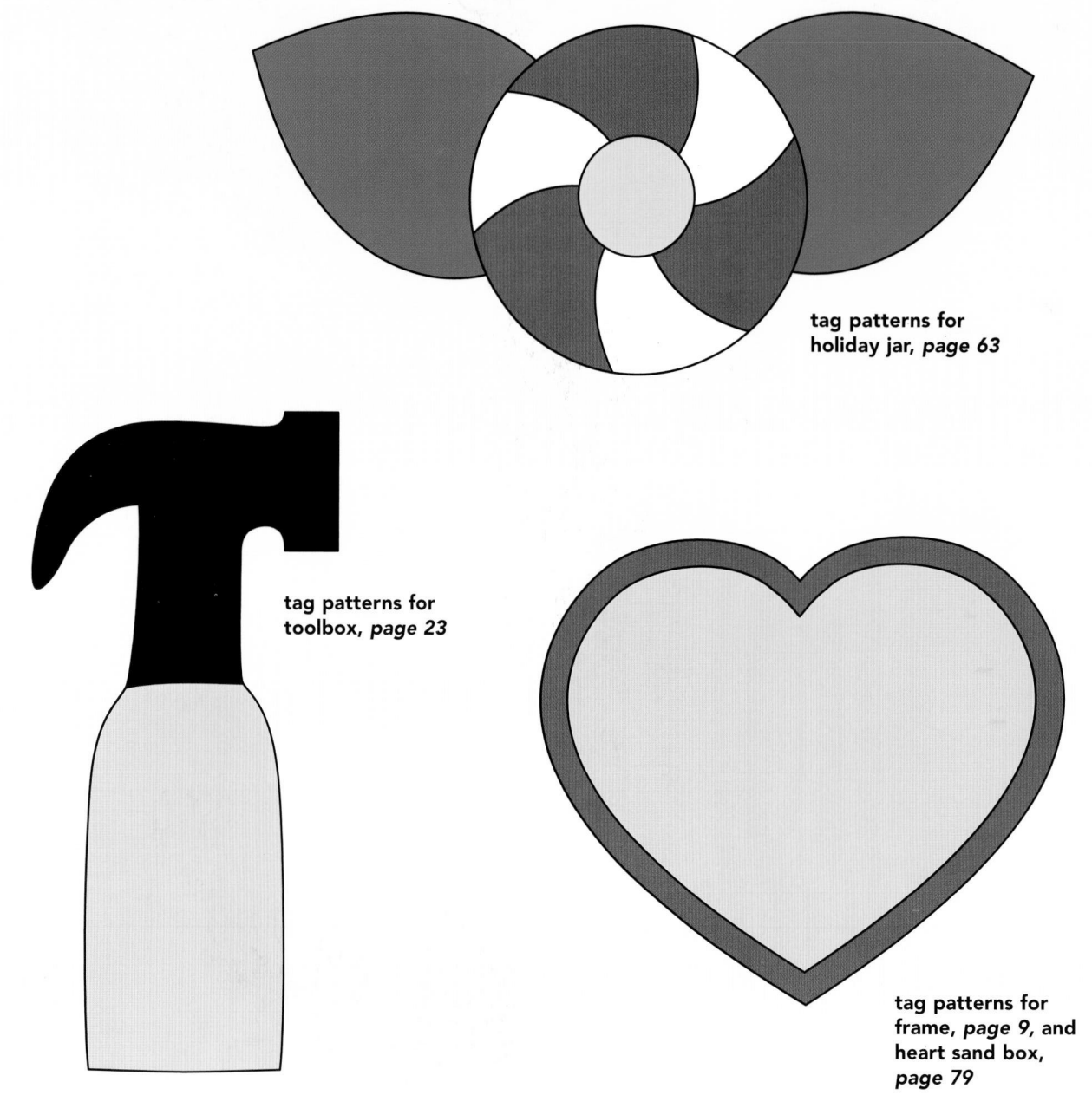

tag patterns for
holiday jar, *page 63*

tag patterns for
toolbox, *page 23*

tag patterns for
frame, *page 9*, and
heart sand box,
page 79

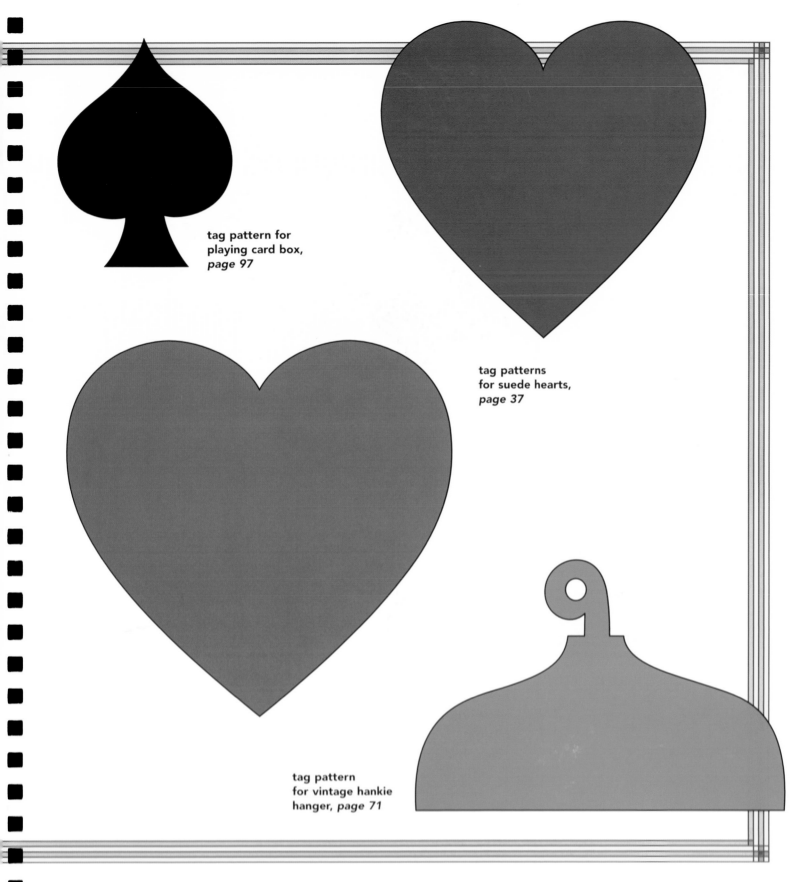

tag pattern for
playing card box,
page 97

tag patterns
for suede hearts,
page 37

tag pattern
for vintage hankie
hanger, *page 71*

Index